AF560844

SCIENCE FICTION

FANTASY AND REALITY

SCIENCE FICTION

FANTASY AND REALITY

Ratnakar D. Bhelkar

PUBLISHERS & DISTRIBUTORS (P) LTD

Published by

ATLANTIC

PUBLISHERS & DISTRIBUTORS (P) LTD

7/22, Ansari Road, Darya Ganj,
New Delhi-110002
Phones : +91-11-23273880, 23275880, 23280451
Fax : +91-11-23285873
Web : www.atlanticbooks.com
E-mail : info@atlanticbooks.com

Branch Office
5, Nallathambi Street, Wallajah Road,
Chennai-600002
Phones : +91-44-64611085, 32413319
E-mail : chennai@atlanticbooks.com

Copyright © The Author, 2009

ISBN 978-81-269-1036-6

All rights reserved. No part of this publication may be reproduced, stored in a retrieval system, transmitted or utilized in any form or by any means, electronic, mechanical, photocopying, recording or otherwise, without the prior permission of the copyright owner. Application for such permission should be addressed to the publisher.

Printed in India at Nice Printing Press, A-33/3A, Site-IV, Industrial Area, Sahibabad, Ghaziabad, U.P.

Foreword

Despite the fact that H.G. Wells, Olaf Stapledon, Aldous Huxley, C.S. Lewis, George Orwell, Arthur C. Clarke and J.G. Ballard are writers of science fiction, it is surprisingly rare that they are considered together at length. It is one of the strengths of the present work that this juxtaposition makes perfect sense, in considering how British science fiction developed as a mode which drew upon techniques of fantasy and realism to comment upon internal and external realities.

Science fiction exists both as a particular response to a literary "moment" (usually speculations about the effect upon society of specific scientific, technological, or sociological changes) and as a general mode of literary expression: part of a wider spectrum that we call the fantastic. In other words, science fiction is both—realistic because it is concerned with the world we know and experience—and non-realistic because it tells that "world we know" by means of the tools of imagination, speculation, fantasy and dream.

The characters of a "realistic" novelist may well experience their world through all these imaginative tools, and more, but we are meant to assume that this world is bound by the same laws as ours. We cannot make the same assumption of a fantasy novelist. Whether it is J.R.R. Tolkien or Terry Pratchett, the point of their imagined "secondary worlds" is that they are not ours and that we can view our own through the lens of the magical and strange. Science fiction is trickier: it is equally a literature of "estrangement" (Tolkien's "arresting strangeness" in his essay "On Fairy Stories" is not, in essentials, so very different from Darko Suvin's "cognitive estrangement") but it both assumes a connection with our real world and questions it. A science fiction may, like Wells's *The Time Machine*, extrapolate a far future, based upon the initial conditions of the author's present, or, like Olaf Stapledon's *Star Maker*, suggest that what we think of as the "laws of the universe" are limited by our fragile perceptions, or, as in J.G. Ballard's early novels, apply metaphorical, symbolic techniques within the context of conventional scientific realism.

As Ratnakar Bhelkar points out, "On the one hand, SF points to fantasy, and, on the other to reality."

One of the apparent paradoxes of science fiction is that its great progenitor H.G. Wells came, in his preface to the 1933 collected *Scientific Romances*, to argue that his early works were not exercises in projecting serious possibilities but "fantasies . . . [that] aim indeed only at the same amount of conviction as one gets in a good gripping dream" (vii). But Wells's "fantasies" were, as the Russian author Yvgeney Zamiatin was to note in his writing on Wells, logical fantasies ("logical fantasy", it might be noted in passing, was the preferred term of John Wyndham for *The Day of the Triffids* and its successors). The hypothesis must be "domesticated" and, as Bhelkar notes below: "Wells creates a fantastic object (say, a time machine) and makes it acceptable to the reader by rooting it in the rational grounding of scientific discourse and concentrating on familiar details such as the *sensations* the Traveler feels as he journeys through time." Wells called this process "an ingenious use of scientific patter" (viii) and "the magic trick" (ix) but we might take these images from stage conjuring one step further and explore Wells's uncharacteristic modesty. We know that the magician's sleight of hand is not magic: we are well aware when we see a conjuring trick that we are being fooled. Our pleasure is in the sense of wonder raised by the illusion itself. When we read a scientific romance, or a science fiction, our pleasure is heightened by the way we can discern the familiar in the strange. We shudder at the Martian monstrosities and the devastation rained down upon the earth by Wells's imagined new weapons of mass destruction, but we remember the novels in which these inventions appear because they extrapolate our collective anxieties.

Hypothesis, extrapolation, sense of wonder—these are all characteristics of the scientific approach Wells grew up with, and may be seen in embryo, in Mary Shelley's *Frankenstein*, that fiction of "ardent curiosity". His successors as novelists in the tradition of the scientific romance, and the "science fiction" crystallized in the American magazines following the publication of Hugo Gernsback's *Amazing Stories* in 1926, drew upon his example. Olaf Stapledon's epic future-history *Last and First Men* is Wellsian—both in its rejection of the adventure-story model *Amazing* fell into (Stapledon, in fact, was largely unaware of the American tradition and almost painfully polite when asked what he thought of it by a science fiction fan in 1937) and in its attempt to extrapolate from the mundane historical facts of its author's present. Stapledon, though, surpassed Wells in his exploration of meaning and metaphysic. The astonishing *Last and First Men* and *Star Maker* are hardly even to be described as novels. Stapledon described *Last and First Men* as an exercise in myth creation, an attempt to chart the spiritual and pragmatic poles of human thought and the apparent conflict between a materialist science and a transcendent religion by means of describing that vast unexplored territory—the future.

Huxley's future is far less ambitiously charted, but it is meticulously charted. The expression "Brave New World" is today far more a reference to Huxley than to Shakespeare; a tribute to the way Huxley built upon the potential of the world he lived in to become what we recognize as what we mistrust in our own. As with Wells, the question of whether Huxley foretold this or that particular element of Planet Earth in the 21st century is beside the point, but his use of devices like biotechnology, social conditioning, and the use of pleasure as a means of control is rooted in his desire to offer plausible extrapolation of what he considered to be our greatest danger—our desire for utopia. In using Wells's extrapolative techniques against him to attack what he saw as Wells's shallow utopianism, Huxley sharpened the use of fantasy for satire, just as Stapledon had grounded his own search for meaning in a mythic extrapolation of the dynamic between the "spiritual" and the "physical".

Ratnakar Bhelkar rightly draws our attention to C.S. Lewis's critical work on science fiction as well as his *Out of the Silent Planet* trilogy, and his determination to echo Stapledon's techniques in responding to his "desperately immoral outlook". While some of us might consider Lewis's response unfair (there are certainly mean-spirited caricatures in *That Hideous Strength*), it is one which has to be made, and Lewis, moreover, had the intellectual tools to make it. While his "scientific patter" fails to reach a Wellsian standard of plausibility, Lewis's background as a medievalist, knowing how symbolism and allegory worked, and his appreciation of science fiction (rare among academics of his time) enabled him to understand how the fantastic and mythic had never gone away. SF as "an imaginative impulse as old as the human race working under the special conditions of our own time" was, for Lewis, the natural vocabulary for what he called "Eschatological fiction". As a Christian, his notion of Eschatology was violently at odds with that of agnostics like Stapledon and Arthur C. Clarke, but the fact that he read Stapledon, and corresponded in guardedly friendly terms with Clarke, argues that while he disagreed with their political/theological means and ends, their literary tools and goals were congenial to him. Particularly in *That Hideous Strength*, he attempts to undermine what he saw as the agenda of other branches of SF, such as that which propagandized for the conquest of space, worlds without end by applying the fantastic against itself. What turns out to be supernatural fantasy attacks the world view of so-called "rational" fantasy, or science fiction. Lewis does not extrapolate, he caricatures, but his command of the language of symbolism and fantasy is what gives his argument the status of myth.

Which leads us to what is here called the "thin"-ness of fantasy in Lewis, and Orwell's *Nineteen Eighty-Four*. Particularly in the latter, "one gets the strong feeling of reality and not of fantasy. One may doubt whether it can be called fantasy." While Lewis's fantasy is designed to lead us towards what might be considered a deeper level of metaphysic (or a truer "inner reality"), Orwell's secular dystopia extrapolates from the political realities of the immediate post-War stand-off between Great Powers and the drive, as he sees it, towards totalitarianism. Lewis warns us against following a particular path. Orwell shows us the result of blindly travelling down another, and his fantasy is so suffused with "confrontation" that our attention passes through it to rest upon the features of the Oceania totalitarianism that we can see in actuality or in potential, in our world. Orwell, too, understands allegory, as *Animal Farm* shows us; the power and horror of *Nineteen Eighty-Four* is that so much of what might be called fantasy is recognizable.

Writing not long afterwards, Arthur C. Clarke, more than any other writer discussed here, might be said to use the language of genre science fiction. The American pulp magazines affected him as much as his early discovery of Olaf Stapledon. Yet here too the tension between what is described and how it is described can be seen. *Childhood's End* is as sophisticated a dissection of utopia as anything by Huxley or Stapledon. The alien "Overlords" bring about beneficial change in a world heading for chaos, and they and the universe they spring from are filled with enough sense-of-wonder for any reader of *Famous Fantastic Mysteries*, in which the early section "Guardian Angel" first appeared in 1950. But this is, first, an imposed utopia and, second, only a provisional one, a stage in the transcendence of the human form. An elegiac tone, so common in Clarke, suffuses everything. If utopia involves sweeping away the past, here the past cannot be relinquished. Bhelkar notes, paraphrasing Clarke: "There are new bridges over the Thames, but in the old places. Nelson's solitary eye still stares down Whitehall's; the dome of St. Paul still stands above Ludgate Hill." And, Clarke concludes, "[t]he guard still marched in front of Buckingham palace." One senses that much as though he desperately wants a universe of space-travel and aliens (and, as he showed us in *Prelude to Space* in 1951, a British presence in opening up this universe) he cannot relinquish the old tribal icons. The physical form of the Overlords suggests an ironic internal reality.

Clarke's scientific and hard SF writing background allowed him to imagine the reality of things—like the surface of other worlds—no one had as yet seen. The imaginations of two visionaries—Arthur C. Clarke and Stanley Kubrick—combined to produce what is still perhaps the greatest "realistic" picture of space travel yet produced, *2001: A Space Odyssey*. Even now, forty years after its release, the film sums up the popular image of space travel. Its future is one where we may be amazed by the wonders which are displayed, yet the journey to the moon is a mundane experience, even boring. Yet just as Clarke makes the strange familiar, so he confronts us with the unknowable that can only exist in the symbolic form of the black monolith. Descriptive language itself breaks down in the face of true "Otherness". We can reconstruct the narrative of the later version of the Overlords who guide human evolution, but Clarke's realistic techniques fail to reproduce the true numinous experience of their existence, motives and goals. There are limits to human comprehension.

How can we comprehend the Alien when we have not understood ourselves? It is perhaps for this reason that Ballard, in his famous editorial to *New Worlds* 118 in 1962, called for an abandoning of stories about the "space age" and demanded "Which Way to Inner Space?"

"Exploring the inner world of man is far more important task for a science fiction writer than portraying outer space." Ballard's characters are often scientists, and his language is frequently richly dense with scientific language, but the terms are taken from psychology and biology (Ballard studied medicine at university) rather than astronautical engineering or physics, and their symbolic meaning is stressed as much as their literal ones: "each nexus of neurones of each spinal level making a symbolic station, a unit of neuronic time". In *The Drowned World* and other early novels drawing upon the tradition of the British "disaster" science fiction, Ballard presents a series of concretely described interior landscapes, often, especially in the short stories of the 1960s, decorated with the surreal images (crashed aircraft, abandoned swimming pools) that we learned in the "realistic" novel *Empire of the Sun* have specific antecedents in "real life".

Science Fiction: Fantasy and Reality offers us first, an approach to the "two faces" of science fiction—its essential dynamic between mimetic and non-mimetic ways of representing reality—and second, a way of moving beyond a conventional history of British science fiction that is either too indebted to the American pulps or refuses to admit their existence. The Wells-Stapledon-Clarke thread in particular would weave back and forth across the Atlantic if we were to consider wider influences, but to note Huxley, Lewis, Orwell and Ballard as well raises fascinating questions about what we mean by pointing to "science fiction" as a genre. All these writers are engaged with reality—not just abstract questions of "meaning" but (albeit from widely differing standpoints) how we confront the future. Their use of fantasy not only illuminates their reactions to their times, but also to each other; and how we may use fantasy to create an "estranged" picture of the world we know, or to move beyond it. The dynamic between these impulses has reverberated for over a century, and shows no sign of dying down.

Andy Sawyer

University of Liverpool, UK

Science Fiction Foundation Collection.

Reviews Editor

The International Review of Science Fiction.

Preview

Science Fiction: Fantasy and Reality is a welcome addition to SF studies in India. It is truly a rare event in the Indian SF scene—the publication of SF criticism by an Indian scholar. In my almost three and a half decades of research effort I have finally seen the light of day.

The book is a "sign of times", also, a timely publication. Interest in SF studies is growing at jet, in India (while it is at hyperspeed in the West). For an SF scholar like me, who has struggled for many years to popularize SF in this country, any speed of growth in SF studies is welcome, and it is fulfilling to see my, often frustrating, efforts fructifying in book term.

One other satisfying aspect of Ratnakar D. Bhelkar's work is the main focus—fantasy. SF studies in India mainly deal with the scientific or the machine-metaphysique themes. Perhaps this is due to some of our early work on Issac Asimov : my doctoral work, one of the first in this country from the University of Madras, was on Asimov's apocalyptic rendition of his messianic robot, Daneel Olivaw, in his foundation universe; Dr. J. Paneerselvam's doctoral work on Asimov's foundation series from a system analysis perspective; and Dr. M.H. Srinarahari's Ph.D. thesis on Asimov's robots. Thus, popular SF themes became the dominant explorations in SF studies. But the fantasy part is rarely touched upon. In fact, at the very first conference that I had organized in 1999 under aegis of the just launched Indian Association for Science Fiction Studies, I was requested by a young enthusiast to include fantasy as a special focus in the next conference. And the writer has made fantasy focus his central issue, showing the other side of science fiction.

It is a matter of pride for me to see that *Science Fiction: Fantasy and Reality* has brought science fiction and fantasy together, in terms of fantasy and reality. This is what I see in the title. Bhelkar has gone and taken us beyond science fiction, to fantasy! And he has achieved this by bringing together, judiciously, some of the most acclaimed SF writers of all times. He has also put SF writers in revealing partnership: H.G. Wells, Aldous Huxley, George Orwell, J.G. Ballard, Olaf Stapledon, C.S. Lewis, and Arthur C. Clarke. The works under discussion are surely some of the most readable SF, classics by their own merit, and enjoying enduring popularity. Apart from being iconic texts in SF genre, they are the best of their authors' creative enterprises. And equally significant is their successful suitability for this book's interpretative efforts.

Ratnakar D. Bhelkar deserves appreciation and plaudits for his bold endeavour in the form of a book on SF and fantasy. Atlantic Publishers too should be congratulated for bringing out the book. Undoubtedly, this volume will be highly useful to scholars and reading public in India and abroad. The book marks an advancement in the field of SF studies in India.

K.S. Purushothaman
Principal
Govt. Arts College, Dharmapuri, Tamil Nadu.
Founder President
Indian Association for Science Fiction Studies, Vellore.

Preface

I had the privilege to study science and literature at the university level, and during that period of study, a thought was knocking at the doors of my mind that there ought to be a sort of relationship between science and literature though they seem diagonally opposite on the surface. Science concerns with facts, reasons, cause and effect and literature too deals with facts but in it facts are presented in modified forms. I thought literature can make use of the knowledge of science to provide novelty to it. In 'The Love Song of J. Alfred Prufrock' T.S. Eliot writes:

> Let us go then, you and I
> When the evening is spread out against the sky
> Like a patient etherised upon a table.

These lines haunted me like Tom Piper's magic whistle because of the novelty of the comparison. I was fascinated when I read the science fictional works of Jules Verne and H.G. Wells, especially because of ideas like the journey to the centre of the earth, the travel into the future, the invisibility of man, with the base of science. Besides the novelty of such thoughts, an idea also struck my mind that Science Fiction (SF) has also a serious purpose, and it has a deeper meaning to unfold. When I visited British Council High Commission Library, Bombay in 1989, I read the book, *Science Fiction: Its Criticism and Teaching* by Patrick Parrinder, and it was a stepping stone to pursue a study in the realm of SF.

In its initial phase, SF was criticised as a brash, emotionally dry, and a commercial form which appeared in pulp magazines, but today it is an established genre of fiction. Readers from different spheres of life are turning to it as an important "sign of times". On the one hand, SF points to the existing corpus of knowledge and on the other, at the fictional world. Fantasy and reality are the cordial components in SF and the present endeavour is directed to explore the relationship between fantasy and reality in their manifestations in SF from 1890s to 1960s. To avoid the topic from becoming unwieldy, only the major SF writers have been selected for the exploration, taking into account the significant contributions they have made to this genre. It was a challenge and yet a pleasant experience to work on this area of the study.

The present work would not have been completed without encouragement and co-operation from the academia and naturally, it is my moral duty to acknowledge the same. First of all, I acknowledge my debt to my research guide Dr. J.B. Paranjape, Professor and Head, Postgraduate Department of English, Nagpur University, who has been a constant source of inspiration and encouragement to me. His insight into criticism and the illuminating hints have helped me to fulfil my cherished dream. I am particularly thankful to him for snatching some precious moments from his hectic academic schedule. I am also thankful to Dr. V.R. Kanadey, former Head, and Dr. (Mrs.) Shernawaz Buhariwala, Reader, Dept. of English, P.G.T.D., Nagpur, for their motivation and suggestions. The fruitful discussion with Dr. Issac Sequaria, Academic Fellow, American Studies and Research Centre, Hyderabad and his valuable suggestions facilitated my journey through the galaxy of British SF writers. I acknowledge the help and assistance rendered by the librarians and the staff members of ASRC, Hyderabad, British Council High Commission Library, Mumbai; British Council Library, Pune; Central Institute of English and Foreign Languages, Hyderabad; Osmania University Library, Hyderabad; University Library, Nagpur; and Ramkrishna Mission Library, Nagpur.

When I was facing the problem of non-availability of some titles, especially by J.G. Ballard, my students, Sachin Date, Mumbai; Tirthankar Bhattacharya, Kolkata; and Buddhaslitta Bose, New Delhi, searched them out from the British Council High Commission Library, Mumbai; National Library, Kolkata; and Jawaharlal Nehru University Library, New Delhi. The discussion I had with my friend Dr. N.Y. Khandait on the topic was an enlightening experience. Although these friends did not expect me to say in words how much I owe to them, I express my thanks to them all for the interest which they have shown in my research work. I owe much to Andy Sawyer whose critical insight into science fiction studies immensely helped me and for his timely Foreword which evaluates *Science Fiction: Fantasy and Reality* in wider perspective. I extend my sincere thanks to Dr. K.S. Purushothaman for his untiring efforts to provide platform to SF enthusiasts and for his Preview, which reveals his depth of understanding and unfolds nuances in SF studies. I am thankful to Dr. M. Narendra and Dr. M.S. Rama Murthy for their enlightening suggestions and warm responses which facilitated the current venture of publication. My brother, Prabhakar D. Bhelkar deserves special thanks for his encouragement to boost my enthusiasm. I extend my thanks to Sangeeta R. Bhelkar for her endurance and assistance and Dr. Meera Singh for momentum and co-operation rendered in this endeavour.

Ratnakar D. Bhelkar

Contents

Foreword .... *v*

Preview .... *xiii*

Preface .... *xv*

1. Introduction 1

2. H.G. Wells 18

3. Olaf Stapledon and Aldous Huxley 37

4. C.S. Lewis and George Orwell 71

5. Arthur C. Clarke and J.G. Ballard 93

In Retrospect 126

Select Bibliography 128

Index 135

Introduction

1

The purpose of this chapter is mainly to answer the theoretical questions : to know what Science Fiction (SF) is and what role fantasy plays in it. Similarly, an acquaintance with theoretical approaches to fantasy may help us to realise its role as mode of thinking in SF. Science is an integral aspect of life in the twentieth century which has witnessed the fundamental metamorphosis in the patterns of life as a consequence of scientific and technological developments. SF has two faces one pointing to the world of fantasy and other to reality. The two elements, fantasy and reality chiefly control the thematic content of SF. The purpose of the present undertaking is to explore the relationship between fantasy and reality in the major British SF from 1890 to 1970 in their diverse manifestations. Herein an attempt has been made to find answer to the following questions: (1) Why does a writer create fantasy? (2) How does a writer make fantasy acceptable to the readers? and (3) What is a writer's approach to reality?

The period 1890 to 1970 is selected for the exploration because SF acquired an independent status as a genre with the novels of H.G. Wells who was a pivotal figure in British SF from 1890 to 1914. In 1964, Michael Moorcock's editorial writings in *New Worlds* paved a way for the emergence of the 'New Wave' in British SF. J.G. Ballard, a leading British SF writer in 1960s anticipated Moorcock's clarion call by creating the apocalyptic SF, and shaped the 'New Wave' in this way. The 'New Wave' preceded British SF after 1960s.

During the Victorian England, the Industrial Revolution accelerated the transformation in the material aspects of human life. The steady flow from the rural, agricultural setting to an urban factory-based environment had brought about a significant change in the way of life in England. Alongside came a new awareness of life. The works of Eramus Darwin on Natural History, Dalton on atom, Mesmer on animal magnetism, and Galvani on bio-electricity contributed significantly to it. Mary Shelley's *Frankenstein* (1818) is an important SF, which owes to the scientific speculation of its time, the researches on bio-electricity, and bases itself on the hypothetical assumption regarding an animated monster. Stevenson's *The Strange Case of Dr. Jekyll and Mr. Hyde* (1866) is a fictional representation about the ambivalence of human nature, and in it Dr. Jekyll, the epitome of victorian respectability, transforms himself into the shape of the criminal Hyde as a result of taking a chemical concoction. After Mary Shelley and Stevenson, H.G. Wells, Aldous Huxley, Arthur C. Clarke, contributed significantly to British SF. In the modern time, SF came to be recognised as a distinct literacy genre, and it is important to know various distinctive features of SF.

(A) Literature of Change

SF presents wonder, action and romance and performs its role as literature of change. As Arthur C. Clarke in his 'Kalinga Award Speech' explains it, the SF writer "by mapping out possible futures as well as a good many impossible ones...encourages in his readers flexibility of mind, readiness to accept and even welcome change—in one word, adaptability."[1] The SF writers have focused attention on overpopulation, pollution, ecological imbalance, automation, mind manipulation, transplantation of tissues, travel in space, encounter with aliens etc.

(B) Dependence on Science

The SF writers create a non-existent condition on the basis of the hypothesis or the primary assumption or the basic premise which is based on accepted principle, a fact in science. "What-happens-if..." approach is basic to the most SF. Essential to SF are scientific or technological instruments. SF often transports a character to the other world, but the entry to the other world is always dependent upon a scientific or technological device. The central concern, however, remains the effects of science on man. Ben Bova observes "Perhaps this is the ultimate role of SF to act as an interpreter of science to humanity.... Only knowledgeable people can wisely decide how to use science and technology for humankind's benefit."[2]

(C) Predominance of Ideas

The most characteristic feature of the genre is the predominance of ideas over everything else. The plot stands or falls by the idea. Characters themselves are sometimes ideas personified, and the narration is the exposition of an idea which is drawn almost exclusively from the sciences–physics, chemistry, biology and geology and their applications in science and techonology.

(D) Extrapolation

SF is frequently set in the future and has often been called 'Futuristic Fiction.' This rests on the effects of science and techonology on man in future. Sam Lundwall writes:

> SF does not predict the future, except accidently. It extrapolates, it amplifies, it magnifies. It deals with changes, the nature that inevitably must change our world whether we like it or not. How we will react to these changes, and how they will effect our lives, that is the rub.[3]

SF extrapolates scientific, social or political changes related to the present time into future. Ben Bova views that SF opens as many futures as possible for man, and states "SF writers are not in the business of predicting future. They do something much more important. They try to show the many possible futures that lie open to us."[4] The common denominator of these views is the orientation to the future, the foreseeing capacity of SF for the possible effects of science and technology upon man, or as Mark Rose writes, "the taste, the feel, the human meaning of scientific discoveries."[5]

(E) Symbol, Metaphor, Allegory

SF yields its meaning when we consider its devices and artifacts as symbols of wish fulfillment, hope, anxiety and fear; its altered settings and alien characters as metaphors of human predicament and manifestations of human nature; its plots as loose allegories of human life.

(F) Modern Mythology

In our own time, when scientific progress and technological advancements have changed the face of the earth, human beings need new myths to explain the inexplicable, to give shape to their unconscious racial and personal obsessions and to recreate their new archetypal images. Sciences have taken the place of old gods in the minds of many people. SF as the literature translating the ideas of science into the fictional situations may be expected to take on the role of the new mythology.

The different distinctive features such as change, dependence on science, predominance of ideas, technique of extrapolation, new symbols, metaphors, and modern mythology based on science, constitute the genre of SF. Different researchers have approached SF taking into consideration some of its distinctive features. Let us examine these various approaches to SF.

In 1926, Hugo Gernsbag, the founder of the first speciality magazine of SF, tried to demonstrate the category "Scientification" (his term for the genre) as "a charming romance intermingled with scientific facts and prophetic vision."[6] By "Scientification", he means the Jules Verne—H.G. Wells—and Edgar Allen poe—type of story, a charming romance intermingled with scientific fact and prophetic vision.

John W. Cambell, the most influential editor that this genre had, wrote in 1952: "Fiction is only dreams written out; SF consists of hopes and dreams and fear (for some dreams are nightmare) of a technologically based society."[7] He proposes that SF should be viewed as a literary medium akin to science itself. Scientific methodology involves a precipitation which not only explains the known phenomenon but also predicts the new and still undiscovered phenomenon. SF tries to do much the same, and hence the preference for the story form.

Kingsley Amis defined SF to an audience of literary scholars at Princeton in 1958 as "that class of prose narrative treating of a situation that could not arise in the world we know, but which is hypothesised on the basis of same innovation in science and technology, or pseudo-science or pseudo-technology, whether human or extra-terrestrial in origin."[8] SF creates a world which may seem impossible, but it is based on scientific ground. The situation may be either human or extra-terrestrial in origin.

Sam Moskowitz considered SF as "a branch of fantasy identifiable by the fact that it ceases the willing suspension of disbelief...by utilizing an atmosphere of scientific credibility for imaginative speculation in physical science, space, time, social science, and philosophy."[9] This view envisages that SF is related to fantasy. The two important aspects of SF are willing suspension of disbelief and scientific credibility.

Robert A. Heinlein, in his essay, 'Science Fiction: Its Nature, Faults and Virtues' defines SF as "realistic speculation about possible future events based solidly on adequate knowledge of the real world, past and present, and one through understanding of the nature and significance of the scientific method."[10] According to him, SF deals with realistic speculation about possible future in scientific way. It is based on the adequate knowledge of the real world.

Darko Suvin, in his essay 'On the Poetics of the Science Fiction Genre', argues for a concept of SF as the literature of cognitive estrangement. To him "SF is then a literary genre whose necessary and sufficient condition are the presence and interaction of estrangement and cognition, and whose main formal device is an imaginative framework alternative to the author's empirical environment."[11] The cognitive element in SF is provided by empirical reality in human world, principles, facts in sciences. Darko Suvin thinks that "'Cognition' does not merely imply reflecting 'of' but also 'on' reality. It implies a creative approach tending towards a dynamic transformation rather than towards a static mirroring of the author's environment."[12] Reflection on the author's empirical environment creates the world of estrangement. The use of estrangement is also found in myth, but, unlike myth, SF sees the norms of any age, including emphatically, its own as unique, and therefore, subject to cognitive glance. The attitude to estrangement comprises factual reporting of fiction with a point of view or glance implying a new set of norms.

The different approaches to SF unfold that on the one hand, SF points to fantasy, and, on the other to reality. It is important to point out here that reality is understood in different ways. The practitioners of the mimetic mode narrates the familiar, usual, known experiences, strictly adhering to facts, and faithfully represents the outside reality. The stream of consciousness writers asserted that reality is in a state of flux, and they tried to give a moment to moment record of changing reality. To them, reality is not static but dynamic. The psychological novelists like D.H. Lawrence used traditional techniques to explore psychological reality by focusing on that part of human personality which is submerged in the sub-conscious. To them, reality is internal. We have learned to doubt interpretability of what we see or learn. Scientists have to reconcile themselves to one kind of uncertainty. They cannot fix both position and momentum of an electron anymore than they can pin a butterfly to a cork and still expect to study its flight patterns. Ultra-violet rays are not visible without the help of a spectrometer. Science has made it hard for us to ignore the illusionary nature of our sense data. From the standpoint of psychologists, reality is a name that we give to something which emerges out of the interaction between the inner and the outer, the subjective and the objective. Our normal day to day experiences can be very well narrated in the "realistic terms" ('realism' being understood in the usual sense). However, for the expression of the unfamiliar, unusual and strange experiences such as an encounter with aliens, we need an altogether different mode. That is where the fantasy mode come significantly into play. Fantasy does not copy empirical world but creates a world which follows its own laws. It deals with a world which does not exist in empirical sense; it deals with the unknown, unseen and unfamiliar world.

However, the term, fantasy mode needs not to be viewed reductively; it cannot be understood in the same sense. The SF writers have made an innovative use of this mode, and critics have examined it from variety of angles. Consequently, the different researchers commenting upon SF have approved fantasy in different ways. Let us examine the diverse approaches to fantasy.

The term, fantasy did not enjoy the same status which it does now. There is no exaggeration in saying that SF has sanctified the fantasy mode of writing. As we know, Coleridge uses the term in a slightly disparaging sense, considering it as an inferior mode. The change in our attitude towards fantasy is reflected at the turn of the century when T.E. Hulme said in clear and unambiguous term that "Fancy will be the necessary weapon"[13] of the new age. Our view of fantasy underwent a change when we contrasted it with reality as distinguished from imagination. These new insights were available due to the Freudian approach.

Freud's approach to fantasy is psycho-analytical and he takes into consideration the role of unconscious desires in relation to fantasy. Freud postulated the wide-ranging influence of the unconscious in human behaviour and thus laid the groundwork for psycho-analytic theory which does not deny but stresses the role which fantasy plays in the apprehension of reality. In the essay 'Formulations on the Two Principles of Mental Functioning' (1919), Freud presents his theory of the primacy of fantasy. The sovereign tendency of the primary mental processes which govern the larger part of the unconscious, is to seek pleasure; that is, this processes either strive, independently and immediately, towards the satisfaction of some need, or flee from some pain. Initially fantasy in the form of hallucinatory wish-fulfilment is the sole form of mental activity. The aim of the first psychic activity is to produce a repetition of the perception which is linked with the satisfaction of a need; the psychic activity produces a "perpetual identity" between the hallucination and that which previously brought satisfaction.[14] Thus hallucination turns away from reality and generates a metaphor: the thought is like the external object which satisfies the need. We turn from fantasy towards reality not in conflict but in accord with the pleasure principle; we learn that to satisfy desires we must plan and act, defer immediate gratification. Nonetheless, a residue of hallucinatory activity is split off, and kept from reality-testing, remaining subordinate to the pleasure principle alone. This residual activity, which functions as a compensation for the normal dominance of the reality principle, is fantasy; and it is the artist's special function to indulge in this compensatory activity. Art's special relevance to the relation between fantasy and reality links it with the central issues of psychoanalysis, and makes Freud's assessment of the artist's motives and the function of his products particularly provoking. He writes:

> An artist is originally a man who turns away from reality because he cannot come to terms with the renunciation of instinctual satisfaction which at first demands, and who allows his erotic and ambitious wishes full play in the life of fantasy by makings use of special gifts to mould his phantasies —into truths of a new kind which are valued by men as precious reflections of reality. Thus in certain fashion he actually becomes the hero, the king, the creator, or the favourite he desired to be, without following the long roundabout path of making real alterations in the external world. But he can only achieve this because other men feel the same dissatisfaction, which results from the replacement of the pleasure principle by the reality principle, in itself a part of reality.[15]

In the Freudian sense, an artist does not confront reality but turns away from it into the world of fantasy to gratify his unconscious desires. He identifies an artist's work with imagined gratification; a pretence of actual satisfaction, as in primary fantasy. He equates fantasy with dream which is an alternative, a substitute, a safety-valve to reality, and views it as an escape from reality.

Besides Freud, Rosemary Jackson and Harold Bloom have approached fantasy in psychological terms. Rosemary Jackson speaks of fantasy as "a literature of desire, which seeks that which is experienced as absense and loss." Further she writes:

> In expressing desire, fantasy can operate in two ways (according to different meanings of "express"): it can tell or manifest or show desire (expression in the sense of portrayal, representation, manifestation, linguistic utterence, mention, description) or it can expel desire when this desire is a disturbing element which threatens cultural order and community (expression, getting rid of something by force) in many cases fantastic literature fulfil both functions at once for

> desire can be expelled through having been told of and thus vicariously experienced by author and reader. In this way fantasy literature points to or suggests the basis upon which cultural order rests for it opens up for a brief moment on to disorder, on to illegality, on to that which lies outside the law that which is outside dominant value systems. The fantastic traces the unsaid and the unseen of culture that has been silenced, made invisible, covered over and made "absent."[16]

Jackson stresses fantasy as subversion and as a means for dealing with that which has been repressed and hence in-expressed. She expresses her belief that fantasy, because of its subversive qualities, "may lead to real social transformation."[17]

Harold Bloom focuses on elements, namely, on World-1 in which a writer lives, a writer and his work:

> Fantasy as a belated version of romance promises an absolute freedom from belatedness, from the anxieties of literary influence and originations, yet this promise is shadowed always by a psychic over-determination in the form of fantasy that puts the stances of freedom into severe question. What promises to be the least anxious of literary modes becomes much the most anxious, and the anxiety specifically relates to anterior powers that is to what might call the generalogy of our imagination. The cosmos of fantasy, of the pleasure/pain principle is revealed in the shape of nightmare, and not of hallucinatory wish-fulfilment.[18]

He thinks that fantasy should free the writer from his sense of being a dwarf following giants, although, paradoxically, promised freedom usually elicits extreme anxiety from the writer.

To Tolkien, fantasy is a natural human activity and as such, it engages both the writer and the reader. Tolkien defines the term 'fantasy' as embodying both and views, "the sub-creativity Art in itself and a quality of strangeness and wonder in the expression.... Fantasy (in this sense) is...not lower but a higher form of Art, indeed, the most nearly pure form, and so (when achieved) the most potent."[19] Tolkien, who applied the phrase, "the sub-creative art" to the writing of fantasy, saw such literary creation as the natural outcome of man's natural creative capacity, in no way conflicting with the exercise of his other principle faculty, his reason. As Tolkien asserts:

> It (fantasy) certainly does not destroy or even insult Reason; and it does not either blunt the appetite for, nor obscure the perception of, scientific verity. On the contrary, the keener and clearer is reason, the better fantasy will it make...for creative fantasy is founded upon the hard recognition that things are so in the world as it appears under the sun; as a recognition of fact, but not a slavery to it.[20]

He envisages that fantasy is not opposed to reason, and reason helps to create better fantasy. Here is a paradox, lying in the heart of fantasy, that is, to be able to create an imaginary world, it is necessary to observe logic and inner consistency. In that world, what an author relates consistently seems 'true' and it accords with the laws of that world, and the reader, too, believes in it.

Thomas D. Clareson also views that fantasy is not opposed to rational thought, and interprets fantasy's relation to SF.

> Fantasy—other side of realism, of which SF is the latest expression—has existed side by side with what has come to be called the mainstream—the "realistic", the representational—throughout literature and certainly throughout the history of modern fiction.[21]

To Clareson, fantasy is not a polar opposite of realism, but other side of realism. It has existed side by side with what has been called as 'realistic.' SF with its freedom to create unearthly worlds as well as to explore and distort time and space, may give new vitality to the dream of human experience.[22] The SF writer has to make the imagined world sufficiently representative so that it becomes acceptable to his readers, and the two parallel traditions have to be intermingled and fused together.

John H. Timmerman views that the chief distinguishing trait of the *genre* of fantasy is perhaps an evocation of other world:

> First, the world matches our world in reality. It is not a dream world, a never—never land, but a world in which characters confront the same terms, choices and dilemmas we confront in our world...second, this world is "evoked", or called forth

> for us, and we have to cross the threshold to it in our minds.... Third, the world of fantasy, however, should not be considered an escapist world, but a world in which we live. There is always this reciprocating action in fantasy, an inter-change between two worlds.[23]

Timmerman wants to assert that the world of fantasy is evoked, purposefully created, and it is provided for human beings to apprehend the known world in new perspectives. Readers have to cross boundaries of 'this' world, the known world to enter into 'other world', the unknown world, the world of fantasy. The world of fantasy is not to be considered as an escapist world which has no relation with the world of factual reality in which human beings live. The reason for creating the world of fantasy is to confront more openly and daringly the reality too often ignored in our world.

Ann Swinfen approaches fantasy in relation to the primary world and the secondary world. In a popular type of fantasy set in the primary world—animal fantasy in which animals are given anthromorphic characters and occasionally human are metamorphosed into animals. Swinfen writes:

> From such fantasy located entirely in the primary world, the move is logically to the next stage in obstruction beyond the normal space—time continuum, where the primary world and other worlds are juxtaposed. The secondary world of such pairs of 'worlds in parallel' still maintains close contact with normal experience in the real world and as such it may be distinguished from the secondary world which is no way directly linked with primary experience.[24]

Superficially, at least, the secondary world of fantasy is remote from everyday life. Such distancing may alienate the readers; or, at any rate fail to involve them, may not awake that deeper level of sympathy which is necessary for the proper understanding of that world which the writer intends to create. However, the reader can be involved if that basis of sympathy and identification can be established. The secondary world of fantasy offers unique advantages. The main advantage of the secondary world for such writer is a freedom from the restricting assumptions and realities of the primary world. Moreover, in the context of an independent secondary world, a new corpus of values may be more easily presented. When a writer of fantasy is in full control of his imagination, and not simply soaring off into the void, he uses these marvellous elements for a specific purpose for imaginative enrichment derived from exploring an experience beyond everyday reality; for the realization of some serious intent which lies beyond his fantasy.[25]

As it has been already pointed out earlier while approaching fantasy, Timmerman concentrates on 'other world' and Ann Swinfen on 'the secondary world.' Kathlyn Hume approaches fantasy laying emphasis on world-1 in which the writer lives. She views that fantasy depends on world-1 from which the author selects and mainpulates materials. World-1 provides the author with the assumptions about reality and meaning. She proposes that fantasy is the desire to alter reality out of boredom, longing for something lacking, or need for the metamorphic images that will bypass the audience's verbal defences.[26] She writes:

> Fantasy is any departure from consensus reality, an impulse native to literature and manifested in innumerable variations from monster to metaphor. It includes transgressions of what one generally takes to be physical facts such as human immortality travel faster than light. Telekinesis and like Telepathy, ...[27]

She makes it clear that since departure from consensus reality can only be registered from its appearence in the text, one might at first class her inclusive definition as work-oriented, but "consensus" immediately refers us to both the world of the author and that of the audience. Here 'consensus reality' means reality which is accepted by the inhabitants of world-1. She includes in fantasy some technical or social innovations which have not yet taken place, even though they may well happen in the future. She also includes in fantasy the alternative worlds and universes, and those stories whose marvel is considered 'real' although not in the same fashion that a chair is real.

These diverse approaches to fantasy reveal that we cannot approach the relation between fantasy and reality in a fixed way. This theoretical discussion about the inter-relation of fantasy and reality is indeed illuminating and valuable. However, there is no fixed theory which can account for the way in which fantasy and reality become operative in different SF. There is no reason why we should follow the preconceived notion about the inter-relation between the two to study British SF.

A brief review of researches in the field may help us to adjust the focus of our inquiry. Those who carried out their research on SF are J.O. Bailey, D.V.K. Raghavacharyulu, David Norman Saumelson. In 1934, J.O. Bailey in his study, *Scientific Fiction in English, 1817—1914: A Study of Trends and Forms,* traced the influences of Jules Verne and Darwin's Theory of Evolution on British SF. His study reveals that British SF from 1817 to 1914 is marked by utopain and satirical elements. According to him, Wells was always interested in the social consequences of advancing science and his interest not only gave his 'scientific fiction' thoughtful substance but led him into his later fields of utopian and sociological writing. The writers of Scientific Fiction have extended the travelogue beyond the confines of the earth, and the historical romance into the future. A widening knowledge of science in the nineteenth century and a deepening faith in it as wonder works have prepared men mind to include these realms of space and time within the area of imaginative art. The seriously written utopias, utopiastic satires, historical romances, and attempts to see man from a viewpoint outside man's spring from the desire not only to escape the world as it is, but to change it. In this respect they differ from other literary avenues of escape.

In 1965, D.V.K. Raghavacharyulu in his study, *Utopia: The Quest and the Crisis* concluded that Utopia as a characteristic literary form, freely combines and integrates into its own organic symbolic modes the varying techniques of fiction and satire, realism and allegory, romanticism and naturalism. The story of the English Utopia, as it emerges from the individual visions of the writers, is the history of the future, whose patterns are closely related to the constant ebb and flow of the ideas, forces and moods which have determined the actual historical background of English consciousness. The classical motivation of utopia is to present it as a promising prospect of an achieved order of perfection which is superior to the existing order. Thomas More, Bacon, Morris, Wells and Samuel Butler, are all prophets who combine, in their sensibility, moral realism and lyric affirmation, radical thought and active reform, organic vision and vital optimism. With Swift's *Gulliver's Travels* the new content of fiction becomes steadily enlarged. The serialised Wellsian Utopia reveals, then, an evolving social vision reflecting his belief in the impossibilities of science, his fear that science may lead the world to the brink of disaster if placed in the hands of irresponsible men. Wells departs from the old methods of shipwrecks and dreams. By the time we come to Huxley's *Brave New World,* utopia becomes completely fictionalized; it becomes a novel of future. Orwell's *Animal Farm* may be the perfect example of the modern allegory. But *Nineteen Eighty-Four* is no more allegorical. It demonstrates, with unflattering realism raised to the intensity of ominous symbolism, what kind of utopia we would attain. There are two marked tendencies in the evolution of Utopia, a steady increase in the narrative element, and the predominance of satire, which result in the creation of anti-utopia.

In 1969, David Norman Samuelson studied in his dissertation, *Studies in Contemporary American and British Science Fiction Novel,* Clarke's *Childhood End,* Asimov's *Caves of Steel,* Sturgeon's *More Than Human*, Miller's *A Canticle of Leibowitz,* Burdry's *Rogue Moon,* and Ballard's *The Crystal World.* His discussion is an integrated study of multiple aspects—the scientific assumption, the theme and motif, plot, characterisation, point of view, structure and style of the six SF novels. All the six authors make use of traditional patterns of fantasy in their novels. Clarke's novel features utopia, an extra-ordinary voyage, contact with the 'supernatural', and the end of the world. Asimov seems mainly concerned with the pattern of dystopia but there are also suggestions of utopia. Sturgeon approaches the ideal of utopia and divinity and relies to some extent on the machinary of the fairly tale. Miller's novel employs the motifs of dystopia, the marvellous journey, world catastrophe, and suggests as well the concepts of utopia and contact with the supernatural. Burdy's book is primarily based on the extraordinary voyage and its adventures, but it also has overtones of dystopia and the supernatural, and stresses a novel approach to the mythological motif of death and rebirth. Finally, J.G. Ballard presents us with an extraordinary journey, a conception of the end of the world, and suggestions of a kind of utopia or immortality within, dystopia beyond, and the supernatural above his crystalized forest. He shows that at the core of SF, lies a scientific hypothesis based on the assumptions of determination, relativism, and empiricism and the goals of prediction, control and comprehension. The strength and weakness of the *genre,* such as they are, arise out of these assumptions and goals.

This brief review of literature in the field of SF studies reveals that the major areas explored by these writers include trends and forms in SF, the historical survey of SF and the notable contribution of individual writers. Although fantasy and reality have been acknowledged as the two dominant elements in SF, critics have not studied British SF with the special reference to fantasy and reality. These being the cordial elements in British SF, an attempt has been made in the present endeavour to understand the interrelation between the two as revealed in and through the works of the major British SF from 1890 to 1970.

To define a term is to impart some fixity to it. Instead, these basic terms can be retained as open terms so that we know how different meanings grow around them. This changing perspective can help us to understand how these concepts have grown over the years, and how the individual writers have contributed to the complexity of the terms. Each new SF ('new' in the Eliotian sense) explores the hitherto unexplored aspects of the *genre,* thus contributing to its development. Each work may therefore be viewed as definition of the *genre.*

Besides the exploration of the fantasy mode, the stress has been given to know the different aspects of reality perceived by the major British SF writers. The grounds to judge the major British SF are (1) a novelty of fantasy, (2) individualities of the SF writers in understanding reality, (3) contribution by the SF writers in shaping the *genre* of SF. Chapter II focuses attention on the British SF from 1890 to the World War I. In this period, H.G. Wells is the single dominating figure in the British SF, and it was he who explored this new territory, settled it, and further developed it. In view of it, an attempt has been made in the chapter to study the elements of fantasy and reality in *The Time Machine* (1895), *The War of The World* (1898), and *World Set Free* (1914). Chapter III deals with the SF of Olaf Stapledon and Aldous Huxley. The most significant contribution to SF during these years was made by Olaf Stapledon and Aldous Huxley. An attempt has therefore been made to study Stapledon's *Last and First Men* (1930), *Star Maker* (1937), and Huxley's *Brave New World* (1932), *Apes and Essence* (1939). Chapter IV concerns with the SF of C.S. Lewis and George Orwell who comprise the major figures in this period. In this chapter, Lewis's *Out of the Silent Planet* (1938), *That Hideous Strength* (1945), and Orwell's *Nineteen Eighty Four* (1949) have been studied. Chapter V encompasses the period of 1950s and 1960s in which the major British SF writers, Arthur C. Clarke and J.G. Ballard contributed significantly to the *genre*. In this Chapter, an effort has been directed to examine Arthur C. Clarke's *Childhood's End* (1953), *2001: Space Odyssey,* J.G. Ballard's the 'New Wave' SF, *The Drowned World* (1962), *The Drought* (1964), *The Crystal World* (1966). The last Chapter states the conclusion of the present study.

REFERENCES

1. Arthur C. Clarke, *Voices From the Future* (New York: Harper, 1965), p. 164.
2. Ben Bova, 'The Role of SF,' *SF: Today and Tomorrow,* ed. Reginaled Brethor (New York: Harper and Row, 1974), p. 14.
3. Sam J. Lundwall, *SF: An Illustrated History* (New York: Crosset & Dunlap, 1978), p. 11.
4. *Ibid.*, p. 4.
5. Mark Rose, 'Introduction' *SF: A Collection of Critical Essays,* ed. Mark Rose (Eglewood Cliffs, N.J.: Prentice-Hall, Inc., 1976), p. 6.
6. Quoted from Scholes and Rubkin, *Science Fiction: History Science-Vision* (New York: Oxford University Press, 1977), p. 3
7. Quoted from Gunn E. ed. *Road to Science* (New York: American Library, 1979), p. 3.

8. Kingsley Amis, *New Maps of Hell* (New York: Arno, 1974), p. 18.
9. Sam Moskowitz, *Explorers of the Infinite* (West Port, Conn.: Hyperion Press, 1974), p. 11.
10. Robert A. Heinlein, 'Science Fiction: Its Nature, Faults and Virtues' quoted in Basil Davilport, ed. *Science Fiction Novel: Imagination and Social Criticism* (Chicago: Advent Publishers, 1959; rpt. 1969), p. 22.
11. Darko Suvin, 'On the Poetics of the Science Fiction Genre', *College English,* Vol. 34, Oct.-Jan. 1972-73, p. 375.
12. *Ibid.*, p. 377.
13. T.E. Hulme, 'Romantism and Classism' quoted in David Lodge. ed., *Twentieth Century Criticism* (Longman, 1972), p. 103.
14. The Standard Edition of the *Complete Psychological Works of Sigmund Freud* (London: Hogarth Press, 1953-74), Vol. 5, p. 566.
15. *Ibid.*, Vol. 12, p. 224.
16. Rosemary Jackson, *Fantasy: The Literature of Subversion* (London: Methuen, 1981), pp. 3-4.
17. *Ibid.*, p. 10.
18. Harold Bloom, *Agon: Toward a Theory of Revisionism* (New York and Oxford: Oxford University Press, 1981), p. 206.
19. J.R.R. Tolkien 'On Fairy Stories', *Tree and Leaf* (New York: Ballantine 1966), p. 44.
20. *Ibid.*, p. 50.
21. Thomas D. Clareson, 'The Other Side of Realism', ed., *SF: The Other Side of Realism: Essays on Modern Fantasy and Science* (Bowling Green Ohio: Bowling Green University Popular Press, 1971), p. 23.
22. *Ibid.*, p. 25.
23. John H. Timmerman, *Other Worlds: The Fantasy Genre* (Bowling Green University Popular Press, 1983), pp. 49-50.
24. Ann Swinfen, *In Defence of Fantasy: A Study of Genre in English and American Literature Since 1945* (London: Routledge & Kegan Paul, 1984), p. 10.
25. *Ibid.*, pp. 92-93.
26. Kathlyn Hume, *Fantasy and Mimesis: Responses to Reality in Western Literature* (New York: Methuen, 1984), p. 20.
27. *Ibid.*, p. 21.

H.G. Wells

2

I

When Mary Shelley wrote *Frankenstein* (1818), SF had neither a name nor any recognition as an independent form of literature. After Mary Shelley, there was a prolonged gap. The popularity of the form dramatically increased in the later Victorian decades with Stevenson's *The Strange Case of Dr. Jekyll and Mr. Hyde* (1886), and William Morris's *News From Nowhere* (1890). After Mary Shelley, Stevenson and William Morris, H.G. Wells is the pivotal figure in British SF. Wells who began publishing in the mid-1890s attributed an independent status to SF and established it. Mary Shelley planted the flag on the new territories, but Wells explored them, settled them and developed them.[1] This is partly because of his mastery of a range of representative themes of time travel in *The Time Machine* (1895), of biological mutation in *The Island of Dr. Moreu* (1896), of invisibility in *The Invisible Man* (1897), of the alien-invasion in *The War of the World* (1898), and partly because his stories embody a new generic combination. *The Time Machine* portrays the process of evolution to the very end of time. *The Island of Dr. Moreu* is a tale of a scientist who turns animals into men; a comment on the co-existence of the noble ideals and base appetites in the same person. *The Invisible Man* shows how a man who has become entirely different is hounded by the mob to the point of no return, reminiscent of the persecutions of the Frankenstein's monster. *The War of the World* (1898) is a powerful documentary on an imaginary Martian invasion of the Earth as seen by an ordinary Englishman. *The World Set Free* (1914) concerns with the catastrophic world after nuclear warfare, and then the rise of the World State. Besides Wells, Arthur Conan Doyle, the author of the detective stories, turned to SF during the period ranging from 1890 to the World War I. Characteristation coupled with humour and science lifted his *The Lost World* (1912) above the level of an average adventure story. It brings the present into the contact with pre-historic past. Profesor Challenger leads an exploring party to the mountains up the Amazon to fulfil his quest in search of living reptiles who had survived after the Jurassic period. In *The Poison Belt* (1913), he forsees the poisoning of the atmosphere of the earth, and gives a humourous treatment to the catastrophic story. Doyle has used fantasy as a mode, and he has raised the adventure story to the level of SF and incorporated humour in it. The effective use of fantasy as a mode is made by Wells, a single dominating figure in the realm of SF in the period from 1890 to World War I. In this chapter, the following representative fiction, *The Time Machine* (1895), *The War of The World* (1898), *The World Set Free* (1914) have been selected for a detailed exploration.

II

Wells lays stress on the principle of a single premise in fantasy which he explains in his preface to *Scientific Romances:*

> As soon as the magic trick has been done the whole business of fantasy writer is to keep everything else human and real. Touches of prosaic detail are imperative and a rigorous adherence to the hypothesis. Any extra fantasy outside the cordial assumption immediately gives a touch of irresponsible stillness to the invention. So as soon as the hypothesis is launched the whole interest becomes the interest of looking at human feelings and human ways, from the new angle that has been acquired.[2]

The principle of adherence to a single premise seems to Wells the only possible way of giving credibility to the fantastic. The fantastic world, 'where anything can happen,' seems to him simply uninteresting and foolish, and as such, it has no right to exist. He emphasizes upon rigorous adherence to the hypothesis, use of commonplace terms and human touches in fantasy so as to make it acceptable to readers.

In *The Time Machine,* Wells himself makes fantasy acceptable to readers by providing a scientific and rational ground to the hypothesis so that it sounds reasonably rational. The basic assumption in the fiction is that a man travels to a remote future by treating time as the fourth dimension. Length, breadth and height are the other accepted dimensions, and time is an assumed dimension. The narrator rationally argues the possibility of this fourth dimension as under:

> 'Scientific people', proceeded the Time Traveller,... "know very well that Time is only a kind of Space. Here is a popular scientific diagram, a weather record. This line I trace with my finger shows the movement of barometer. Yesterday it was high, yesterday night it fell, then this morning it rose again, and so gently upward to here. Surely mercury did not trace this line in any of the dimensions of Space generally recognised? But certainly it traced such a line, and that line, therefore, we must conclude was along the Time Dimension."[3]

The Time Traveller asserts to the Medical Man and to the Psychologist that there is no difference between Time and any of the three dimensions of space. Our consciousness moves along with it. It is this fantastic assumption which the writer wants his readers to accept without hesitation. Once this assumption is accepted, the writer describes the mechanism of the time machine following a realistic model. The time machine is a glittering metallic framework, scarcely larger than a small clock, and very delicately made. There is ivory in it and some transparent crystalline substance. The Time Traveller says to the Medical man, Filby, psychologist and the provincial Mayor:

> Now I want you clearly to understand that this lever, being pressed over, sends the machine gliding into the future, and this other reverses the motion. This saddle represents the seat of a time traveller. Presently I am going to press the lever, and off the machine go. It will vanish, pass into the future Time, and disappear.... Look at the table too, and satisfy yourselves there is no trickery.(9)

He invests the mechanism of the time machine with precise and familiar details. Besides the realistic description of the mechanism of lever, the fantastic beings, Eloi and the Morlocks, are presented in a realistic way. They have human features like face, hands, legs, body. The eyes of Morlocks are like those of owls and cat.

Nothing serves so well for the authenticity of fantasy as the authenticity of human reactions to the events. The time Traveller's courage, strangeness, fear and anxiety are real. His task to venture into the unknown furture world is adventurous, and he can fulfil his purpose because of his immense courage. When he travels to the future world unknown to him, he experiences strangeness of everything, the sick jarring and swaying of the machine, and above all, the feeling of prolonged falling. When his time machine is lost he becomes helpless in a strange world, and experiences as actual physical sensation in his throat and feels as if his breathing has stopped. As the narrator puts it, "I suppose it was the unexpected nature of loss that maddened me. I felt hopelessly cut off from own kind—a strange animal in an unknown world"(44). He feels like one who is isolsted from human beings on the earth. He is a stranger desirous of visiting some unknown world, he seems to be over-anxious to get out of it. In a colossal ruin near the great house, he notices the glaring eyeballs in the darkness and experiences the terror of darkness. "I was oppresed with perplexity and doubt," he says, "Once or twice I had a feeling of intense fear for which I could perceive no definite reason."(63) Oppressed by perplexity, doubt, and intense fear in the future world, his sense of security is threatened.

Wells makes fantasy acceptable by providing it the rational ground of science and by investing the strange new world with familiar details. While the land remains strange and unfamiliar, the emotions and feelings are maintained at the level of real.

In the last quarter of the ninteenth century, industrialization had received a momentum. Textile mills were opened in Manchester and new industries were launched in urban areas. The age of machines was set in and the process of migration of the rural population to the urban areas was initiated. New products were manufactured and jobs were made available to workers. As a consequence of the rise of industrialization, the two classes, the rich and the poor, the industrialists and the workers were formed in the industrial society of the 1890s. The rich class, the industrialists exploited workers as a consequence of aggregated money power in the hands of the few. Wells is dissatisfied with this aspect of the contemporary reality. Thirty years later, Wells was to define this problem in definite terms:

> There can be little question that the existence of this irresponsible rich class, so conspicuous in contemporary life, involves very considrable waste of human resources, vulgarization of youthful imaginations, and a widespread demoralization of potential producers. Moreover, it carries with it the possibility of powerful, irrational interventions in the political and general mental life of the communtiy.[4]

He isolates this aspect of the contemporary reality—the irresponsibility of the rich class and exploitation of workers and deems it as a significant sign of the time further; he studies its future implications. In *The Time Machine,* he extrapolates his dissatisfaction with contemporary reality in the future society in the year 802,700, and presents us an enlarged, vivid picture of it in a set of two types of creatures who differ from one another in more respects than in what they resemble.

In the future world, the Time Traveller finds mankind housed in splendid shelters. The population is balanced. Diseases are stamped out. There is no danger of war or solitary violence; no danger from wild beasts. He feels: "It was natural on the golden evening that I should jump at the social paradise." Besides these utopain aspects of the future society, the Time Traveller finds men of the eight hundredth millennium beautiful and graceful, but frail and childlike with a "dresden china type prettiness." Evolution has smoothed the features of mankind, but removed strength along with ruggedness. The Eloi, the upper world people, live on the crust of the earth. These people who pursue pleasure, comfort and beauty are the descendants of the present day 'haves.' They can recruit machines to enjoy the life of ease without effort. This very dependence on machine brings about the decay of their powers. They are content to live in ease and delight, making use of the labour of their fellowmen. The narrator observes: "...very pleasent was their day, as pleasent as the day in the field. Like the cattle, they knew no enemies and provided no needs (97)." Assured of their wealth and comfort, they favour aristocracy and exploited their mechanical servants, the Morlocks. The Eloi stand for the industrialists, masters, capitalists and oppressors. The Morlocks are the 'have nots' who become adapted to the conditions of continuous labour. Although they are assured of their lives and their work, they live in caverns inside the earth in inhuman conditions. Thus they are reduced to the level of mechanical servants who are deprived of their spirit. The Time Traveller observes the artificial Under World:

> Beneath my feet, then, the earth must be tunnelled enormously, and these tunnellings were the habitat of the new race. The presence of ventilating shafts and wells along the hill slopes everywhere, in fact, except along the river valley showed however were its ramificatons. What so natural, then, as to assume that it was in this artificial Under-world that such work as was necessary to the comfort of the daylight race was done? The notion was so plausible that I at once accepted it, and went on to assume how of this splitting of the human species (59-60).

In the future world, the earth appears to be enormously tunnelled inside and there are ventilating shafts and wells along the hill shopes. The Time Traveller travels along the tunnel inside and at last sees a vast arched cavern which stretches into utter darkness. The noise of machinary gets louder. The Under-World is stuffy and oppressive as the narrative goes:

> Necessarily my memory is vague. Great shapes like big machines rose out of the dimness, and cast grotesque black shadows, in which dim spectral Morlocks sheltered from the glare. The place, by the by was very stuffy and oppressive, and the fait habitus of freshly shed blood was in the air.... The Morlocks at any move carnivorous (67).

Inside the earth, at depth, the Morlocks live in an abnormal condition. In caverns, they work on machine for the sake of the Upper-World people, the Eloi. They are no better than slaves, subjected to the tyranny of their masters, the Eloi, who enjoy the fruits of their toil. The Morlocks have no freedom whatsoever and it is thought to be the right especially of the Eloi. The Time Traveller sees the exploitation of the Morlocks by their masters:

> They were there, they would no doubt have to pay rent, and not a little of it, for the ventilation of their caverns; and if they

> refuse, they would starve or suffocated for arrears. Such of them as were so constituted as to be miserable and rabellious would die; and, in the end, the balance being permanent, the survivors would become as well adapted to the conditions of underground life, and as happy in their way, as the Upper-World people were to theirs (61).

If the Morlocks refuse to pay money for their residential charges, they are made to starve or sometimes to suffocate for arrears. Their is a miserable condition. If the Morlocks attempt to rebel against the Eloi, an attempt to revolt is suppressed, using an iron hand. In this world, the penalty for revolt is nothing short of death. In contrast to the exploited condition of the Morlocks, the Eloi are free to roam anywhere, and enjoy anywhere. With no work, they live in ease and delight upon the labours of their fellowmen. Commenting upon the anti-utopian form of the future society, Damon Knight Writes:

> From a parodied Morrisite model ("Communism" says the Time Traveller at first sight) through the discovery of degeneration and of persistence of class divisions, he arrives at the anti-utopian form most horrifying to the Victorians a run-down class society ruled by a grotesque equivalent of the nineteenth-century industrial proletariat.[5]

The Time Traveller knows that the roots of the Eloi Morlock situation go back to the slowly widening gap between the 'haves' and 'have nots'. The narrator writes:

> At first, proceeding from the problems of our own age, it seemed clear as daylight to me that the gradual widening of the present, merely temporary and social difference between the capitalist and labourer was the key to the whole position (60).

The Time Traveller is aware of contemporary reality of exploitation of workers, which he observes in the relationship between the Eloi and the Morlocks in the future world, in magnified and intensified form. The two classes, the capitalist and the labour are formed in the future industrial society, and the class division is rigid. He feels that the exploitation of the Morlocks by the Eloi, leading to their degradation to an inhuman level, is the logical culmination of the contemporary reality of the exploitation in the industrial society of the 1890s. Kagarlitsky Yu has rightly pointed out:

> *The Time Machine* was a remarkable triumph for the young satirist. In *The Time Machine,* he depicted the logical consequence of contemporary social and economic order which was gengrally regarded as natural and normal.[6]

To Patrick Parrinder, the Eloi and the Morlocks represent degeneration of human civilization.[7] According to Wells, the class conflicts lead to degeneration of human civilization and degradation of human life. Excessive dependence on machine atrophies human features. The episode of the Eloi and the Morlocks, although a demonstration of evolutionary decline seems to embody a warning of the possible consequence of the greed, complacency, and the rigid class division of the present society. The overall effect of all this is that in this machine age, man's mind weakened.

III

The last decade of the ninteenth century is notable for the scientific advance which was to affect human society. Researches in astronomy have changed some of our fundamental concepts about cosmos. The Victorians were curious about the reddish planet Mars. What made them feel fascinated was the popular belief that there was life on this red planet—a notion which was reinforced by Schiparellis. An interesting account of this intense belief is to be found in Mark Hillgas's article 'The First Invasion from Mars.'[8] Wells accepts the contemporary reality of the popular interest of the Victorian people in Mars and considers it as an important sign of the time. This provides him the necessary excuse for the fantasy in the *War of the World* (1898), which enables him to present it in a magnified form for the purpose of stress.

In the fiction, the Martians, whose motives are quite incomprehensible to man, treat humans as though they were an obsolete race. This Darwinian fable, depicting an interplanetary struggle for suvival, is the most influential of all alien contact stories. The narrator mentions that a great light was on the illuminated part of disc. Hundreds of observers see the flame for ten nights and think of it as the result of some volcanic eruption there. The first cylinder buries in England's sand, gathers to see the 'meteor'. The cylinder is artificial, hollow with an end that screws out. Each cylinder is a monstrous triped, higher than many houses, striding over the young pines and smashing them aside. Triped is a walking engine of glittering metal; articulate ropes of steel dangling from it and the clattering tumult of its passage mingling with the riot of the thunder. The Martians are inside the cylinder, and their peculiar appearance is due to evolutionary changes in their body. Their mouth is surrounded by the tentacles which are used for rapid movement and for blood sucking. Their body organs are modified for practical purposes. The whole complex apparatus of digestion, which makes the bulk of our bodies, does not exist in the Martians. They do not eat, much less digest. Instead, they take the fresh living blood of other creatures, and inject it into their own veins. The physiological advantage of the practice of injecting blood is more if one thinks of the tremendous waste of human time and energy required by digestive process. Men go happily or miserably depending upon whether they have healthy livers or sound gastric glands. But the Martians are lifted above all these organic fluctuations of mood and emotion. They are absolutely without sex, and therefore, without trumultous emotions that arise from the difference among men. For reproduction they follow the budding process. They wear no clothing. They are evidently more sensible to changes of temperature than we are. Changes of pressure do not affect their health seriously. So the Martians are more resistant and more evolved than human beings in some respects. They communicate among themselves with a peculiar sound, "Ulla, Ulla, Ulla." They experience heaviness of movement due to the greater gravitational pull of the earth than that of Mars.

The Martians cause heavy destruction and finally drive human beings to the brink of defeat. A metallic Tripod smites the Heat-Ray out of the funnel. In one night the valley is reduced to ashes. They discharge the Black Smoke by means of rockets. The narrator highlights the mighty strength of the Martians, which are able to paralyse human forces:

> The Martians are able to discharge enormous clouds of black and poisonous vapours by means of rockets. They have smothered our batteries, destroyed Richmond, Kingston, and Wimbledon, and are advancing slowly towards London, destroying everything on the way. It is impossible to stop them.[9]

They are the agents of death. They are not merely a handful of small sluggish creatures, but "they are minds swaying vast mechanical bodies"; and they can move swiftly and smite with such power that even the mightiest guns cannot stand against them. Before the mighty power of the Martians, the human race is feeble. The Londoners are sick of fear; they are strirring, running, and sleeping. The advance scientific and dreadful weapons like 'Black-Smoke' and 'Heat-Ray' prove the superiority in the war power of the Martians against the human race. They destroy the important areas of London, explode stores of gun powder that they come upon; cut every telegraph wire and wreck the railways here and there. Farmers are out to defend their cattle-sheds, granaries, and ripening root crops with arms in their hands. In Sunbury along the roads, there are dead bodies lying in contorted attitudes, horses as well as men, overturned carts and luggage, all covered thickly with black dust. The narrator says: "That pall of cindery powder made me think of what I had read of the destruction of Pompeii (788)." Commenting upon their superb intelligence and the comparative littleness of mankind, Mark Rose writes:

> The contrast between the greatness of the Martian intelligence and the littleness of mankind that dominates the novel's opening recalls the familiar contrast between the greatness of the cosmos and human littleness. Indeed, what Wells has done is to transfer the usual attributes of the physical cosmos—vastness, coldness, indifference – to the Martians. Significantly, the Martians in their fighting machines dwarf men physically, even as their great brains dwarf ours intellectually. Their weapons–the heat ray, the poison gas are depersonalizing instruments of mass slaughter, and attempts to communicate with them are as fruitless as if they are literary a force of nature.[10]

The Martians' reign of horror and terror shocks the people and they imagine what World War I and the post-World War I hold in store for mankind. Wells' concern for civilization is evident from the way he presents the Martians as the advanced race, and man's complacent and confident assumption of future and his place in the Universe is roughly shaken. P.K. Krishnamoorthy observes that Wells's fanatsy in *The War of the World* shows how fragile is the stability of our society in the face of the unknown.[11]

In fantasy, the imperialism of the Martians meets its nemesis at the hands of the terrestrial bacteria against which, they have no immunity. As Patrick Parrinder says, this is by no means a single minded, anti-imperalist tale, since the Martian's path of escape from their native planet is one which mankind must eventually follow.[12] Wells's Epilogue hints strongly that the two races are destined to compete for the mastery of the universe:

> We have learned now that we cannot regard this planet as being fenced in and a secure an abiding-place for man; we can never anticipate the unseen good or evil that may come upon us suddenly out of space. It may be that in the larger design of the universe this invasion from Mars is not without its ultimate benefit for men; it had robbed us of that serene confidence in the future which is the most fruitful source of decadence, the gifts to human science it has brought enormous, and it has done much to promote the conception of the commonwealth of mankind.... It may be, on the other hand, that the destruction of the Martians is only a reprieve. To them, and not to us, perhaps, is the future ordained (827).

The ultimate benefit that the invasion may have brought about is scarcely utopian. Even the 'conception of the commonwealth of mankind' seems to be intended, in this context, only to turn the human race inito a more efficient military unit. To Mark Hillegas, *The War of the World* is obviously intended to attack human complacency, as the narrator himself reminds us while discussing the benefits which "In the larger design of the universe," have come from the invasion.[13]

The desire to rule over others and to subdue others in the very germplasm of living beings whether they belong to the earth or to Mars. That is the reality. Here we have the source of all imperialism which leads to wars. We subjugate others, thinking that we are superior. But, set against a more powerful foe, we appear to be dwarfed. Through fantasy in *The War of the World,* H.G. Wells highlights the insufficiency of the human race which seems helpless against the more powerful foes. In a way, it is a warning aganist complacency and smugness—the typical by-products of the Victorian belief that the scientific advance contains solutions to all problems. We must not forget that human beings on the planet earth are tiny specks in the vast cosmos. He highlights the littleness of mankind in the presence of the mighty, malevolent aliens, and satirises the egoistic tendency of man who thinks that he (man) is the only powerful being in cosmos. Wells hints at 'the commonwealth of mankind'; the urgency of uniting together keeping aside our difference, and avoid a catastrophe for the betterment and upliftment of human society.

IV

The Wold Set Free (1914) was written under the immediate shadow of World War I. In the period prior to World War I, aggressive nationalistic tendenies were receiving momentum; conflicts among nations were increasing. The Emperor Kaiser William made a kind of regal progress through the Holy Land, Landed at Tangler to assure the Sultan of Morocco of his support against the French. In 1908, Austria, with his support, defied the rest of Europe by annexing from the Truck the Yugo-Slav provinces of Bosina and Heozegovina. He forced Britain, France, and Russia into a defensive understanding against him, by offering a naval challenge to Britain and by making agressions upon France and the Slaves. The Bosnian annexation had the further effect of estranging Italy, which had hitherto been his ally.[14] The Great Powers were unwilling to face the prospect of a merger of Sovereign powers, without which permanent peace projects were absurd. There was no ceasation of international competition during the acute phase or war which was becoming too costly. Each wanted to economize minor disputes and conflicts and to formulate international laws that would embarrass the more formidable opponents in war-time without incommoding itself.[15] He was also aware of the two conferences at the Hague in Holland, one in 1899 and another in 1907, to make the great idea of universal peace triumph over the elements of trouble and discord. They were represented diplomatically, and for the most part the assembled representatives hanggled cunningly upon points of international law affecting war, leaving aside the abolition of War as a chimera.[16] Wells is dissatisfied with aggressive nationalistic tendencies, conflicts among nations and unsuccessful ventures to resolve them. He writes in his preface to *The World Set Free:* "Every intelligent person in the world felt that disaster was impending and knew no way of averting it, but few of them realised in the earlier half of 1914 how near the crash was to us."[17] He read Fredrick Soddy's essay, 'Interpretation of Radium' and wrote to his friend Simmons, "My idea is taken from Soddy. Men are supposed to find out how to set up atomic degeneration in the heavy elements just as they found out long ago how to set up burning in coal. Hence, limitless energy."[18] Taking a cue from the experiment on radioactive elements, he individuates his sense of dissatisfaction with reality and extrapolates his sense of dissatisfaction by turning it into fantasy which creates the vivid catastrophic picture of the atomic war, and the world state based on mutual understanding, sympathy, and love for peace and order.

Holsten's research on atomic energy in 1933 was to lead to the manufacture of the atomic bomb. He had set up atomic disintegration in a minute particle of bismuth; it exploded with great violence into a heavy gas having extreme radio-activity, which disintegrated in its turn in the course of seven days. In this process of disintegration of bismuth, the last product was gold, and during the process a lot of atomic energy in machine was released. In 1953, attempts to use atomic energy in machine were successful and the first Holsten-Roberts engine brought induced radio-activity into the sphere of industrial production, and its first general use was to replace the steam-engine in electrical generation stations. Later on it replaced other forms of energy. Highways were thronged with machines that charged a penny to run thirty-seven miles; Redmayne's helicopter, allowing for straight up and down hovering, revolutionized aviation. But those researches brought on social ills : coal mines closed; oil became worthless; the stock market was in a panic. In that period of development of atomic science, relations among nations were more strained. The stumbling blocks were the boundaries of a general predominance in human affairs on the part of some one particular state. Germany was "the heart and centre of Europe."

The central European powers suddenly attacked the Slav Confederacy, and France and England went to the help of the Slavs. Chinese and Japanese attacked Russia, and there was revolutionary outbreak in America. The aggressive nationalism and conflicts among nations resulted into the atomic warfare in 1956 which was unlike the earlier historical wars because for the first time atomic bomb was used in war and its consequences were simply disastrous.

In the atomic war, the lumps of pure carolium, painted on the outside with the unoxidised cydonator inducive enclosed in a case of membrainium were used. A little celluloid stud between the handles by which the bomb was lifted, was arranged so as to easily torn off and admit air to the inducive in order to set up radio-activity in the outer layer of the carolinum sphere. That liberated fresh inducive, and so in a few minutes the bomb was ablazing continual explosion. Atomic bombs which were thrown from aeroplanes fell in this state; they reached the ground still mainly solid and, melting soil and rock in their projects, bored into the earth. Once launched the bomb was absolutely unapproachable and uncontrollable till its forces were nearly exhausted. Such was the crowing triumph of military science, the ultimate explosive that was to give the 'decisive touch' to war. Wells narrates the dire consequences of the atomic explosion:

> For the whole world was flaring then into a monstrous phase of destruction. Power after power about the armed globe sought to anticipate attack by aggression. They went to war in a delirium of panic, in order to use their bombs first. China and Japan had assailed Russia and destroyed Moscow, has United States had attacked Japan, India was in anarchistic

> revolt with Delhi, a pit of fire spouting death and flame: the redoubtable King of the Balkans was mobilising. It must have seemed plain at last to every one in those days that the world was slipping headlong to anarchy. By the spring of 1959 from nearly two hundred centres and every week added to their number, roared the un-quenchable crimson conflagrations of the atomic bombs; the flimsy fabric of the world's credit had vanished, industry was completely disorganised and every city, every thickly populated area, was striving or trembled on the verge of salvation. Most of the capital cities of the world were burning, millions of people had already perished, and over great areas government was at an end. Humanity has been compared by one contemporary writer to a sleeper who handles matches in his sleep and wakes to find himself in flames.[19]

Radio-active vapour drifted sometimes scores of miles from the bomb centre and killed and scorched all they overtook. And the first conflagrations from the Paris centre spreaded westward, half-way to the sea. Moreover, the air in the infernal circle of red-lit ruins and peculiar dryness and blistering quantity, so that it set up a soreness of the skin and lungs that was very diffcult to heal. Such was the state of Paris and such on a larger scale was the condition of affairs in Chicago, and the same fate had overtaken Berlin, Moscow, Tokyo, the eastern half of London, Toulan, Kiel. All the great capitals are struck. As the catastrophe was of considerable magnitude, the questions such as how to end war and how to make mankind survive were of seminal importance. Leblanc, the French ambassador at Washington was instrumental in calling the meet of the chief powers of the world on the Alpine mountain side, to save humanity. He won over the American president and the American government to his humanistic ideas. King Egbert, the young king of the most vulnerable state in Europe, was a rebel against the magnificence of his position, and attended the conference with his secretary, Firmin. King Egbert was nominated as a president of the international conference for peace, by Leblanc. King Egbert said, "The World has been mashed up, and we have to put in on its wheels again." He favoured the idea of the World State and declared, "we have to get every atom of Carolium and all the plant for making it into our control." To Holsten, science was the new King of the world. But king Egbert viewed, "It is that common impersonal will and sense of necessity of which science is the best understood and most typical aspect. It is the mind of the rest. It is that which was brought us there, which was bowed us all to its demands (150)." At the initial level, the King of Balkans debated and delayed his submission to the World Council, but finally he submitted unwillingly. His stock of atomic bombs was seized and in the encounter, he was killed. It ushered into a new phase of human civilization. Everywhere on the world was given a vote and democratic pattern was followed; uninhabited wildernesses were systematically opened up; population was spreaded through the country (for the cities were still exploding craters); the English language, shorn of grammatical varieties was adopted as a world language. Science flowered as a world-wide co-operative enterprise fully supported by the state. Science was something more than "our little individual selves." It was "the awakening mind of the race." Marcus Karenin expressed that the curtain had risen from the gloomy and nightmarish scene of the world:

> Man lives in the dawn for ever,...Life is beginning and nothing else but beginning. It begins everlastingly. Each step seems vaster than the last, and does but gather us together for the next. This Modern State of ours, which would have been a Utopian marvel a hundred years ago, is already the commonplace of life (234).

Wells's optimism about human future is mirrored in the words of Marcus Karenin; the untiring efforts of Leblanc and of King Egbert for humanistic ideals of peace, order and happiness. Fredrick A. Kreuziger has observed that H.G. Wells in narrating how utopia came into existence, "begins with the prediction of the collapse of the present world order, due to the fact that this order remains based on nation-states autonomy long after scientific and technological revolution has rendered that political structure obsolete. In the wake of the inevitable collapse, a world-state Utopia is established."[20] Wells's fantasy of the application of atomic bomb is turned into reality in World War II (1939-45); his idea of World State, harmony, co-operation brotherhood among nations has materialised to some extent in the establishment of United Nations Organisation (UNO) in 1945. The twentieth century has witnessed to more degree, the horrible conseqeunces of dropping of atomic bombs on the Japan's two cities, Hiroshima and Nagasaki in 1945. From this standpoint, Wells's prophetic power keeps parallel with Jules Verne's fantasies which have been turned into reality as in *From The Earth to the Moon* (1865) and *Twenty Thousand Leagues Under the Sea* (1870).

In the preface to *The World Set Free,* Wells has stated his thesis in the following words:

> Because of the development of scientific knowledge, separate sovereign states and separate sovereign empire are no longer possible in the world, that to attempt to keep on with the old system is to heap disaster upon disaster for mankind and perhaps to destroy our race altogether.[22]

His approach to reality is that aggressive nationalism and conflicts among nations lead to war, and application of scientific advancement in war makes war more gruesome and worse, and poses a threat to wipe out human existence. Understanding, sympathy, co-operation and love among nations create the golden era of peace, order and happiness. He warns that the present system, unless it can develop a better intelligence and a better heart, is manifestly destined to face fresh wars and to continue wasting that is left of the substance of mankind, until absolute, social disaster overtake us all. His apocalyptic vision of reality shocks readers who are disillusioned with scientific progress; his utopian vision of reality consoles them.

V

The principle of the single premise seems to Wells the only possible one for fantasy. He emphasises upon rigorous adherence to the fantastic hypothesis, use of commonplace terms and human characteristic in fantasy to make it accepatable to readers. Nothing serves so well for the authenticity of fantasy as the authencity of human reactions to the events. He makes fantasy acceptable to readers by providing the rational ground of science and investing the strange new world with familiar details. While the land remains strange and unfamiliar, the emotions and feelings are real.

Wells envisages the exploitation of workers by irresponsible rich class; the popular interest of the people in the Mars as the abode of life; aggressive nationalism, conflicts among nations, and unsuccessful venture to resolve them, as the important signs of the time. He is dissatisfied with reality and individuates his sense of reality. He does not escape from reality but accepts it and extrapolates it into fantasy, to view it in a new perspective. He uses fantasy as a mode to extrapolate reality, and express his meaning of reality. To Wells, fantasy mode is important in so far as it allows him the necessary freedom to create his world which would embody his vision of reality. In fact, the very problems faced by his contemporaries are presented here in the magnified form so as to highlight the essential elements of reality. For instance, class conflicts lead to degeneration of human civilization; degrade human life and bring it to inhuman level. Excessive dependence on machines atrophies in human features; the Machine Age weakens man's mind. Human beings on thc planet, the earth are tiny specks in the vast cosmos; aggressive nationalism and conflicts among nations lead to war, and application of scientific advancement in war makes war more gruesome and worse, and poses a threat to wipe out human existence. Understanding, sympathy, co-operation and love among nations are necessary for peace, order and happiness in human society. The desire to exploit others is so great that human beings are reduced to the level of mechanical servants, leading a life no better than that of the slaves in the ancient eras. Similarly, the desire to rule over the entire world is so great that the other race finds itself on the brink of extinction. The same desire is at work even in the last novel and ironically enough, the agent of destruction turns out to be a boon in disguise as it compels men to adopt the policy of mutual understanding.

REFERENCES

1. Robert Scholes and Eric Rubkin, *Science Fiction: History-Science-Vision* (New York: Oxford University Press, 1977), p. 15.
2. H.G. Wells, *Preface to Scientific Romances* (London: Gollancz, 1933), p. viii.

3. H.G. Wells, *The Time Machine* (New York: Bantom Books, 1982), p. 4. (all the subsequent quotations are from this edition, and are indicated in parantheses by page number/numbers).
4. H.G. Wells, *The Work, Wealth and Happiness of Mankind* (London: William Heinemann Ltd., 1932), pp. 480-81.
5. Damon Knight, 'Wells as the Turning Point of the SF Tradition' *Turning points: Essays on the Art of SF* (New York: Harper, 1977), p. 212.
6. Kagarlitsky Yu. 'The Summing-Up (H.G. Wells),' *The Twentieth Century English Literature: A Soviet View,* ed., Antoli Moisew (Moscow: Progress Publishers, 1982), p. 52.
7. Patrick Parrinder, *Science Fiction: Its Criticism and Teaching* (London: Methuen & Co. Ltd., 1982), p. 94.
8. Mark Hillegas, 'The First Invasions From Mars' *Michigan Review, LXVI* (February 1960), pp. 107-22.
9. H.G. Wells, *H.G. Wells* (London: William Heinemann Limited, 1980), p. 764 (all the subsequent quotations are from this edition, and are indicated by page number/numbers in parantheses).
10. Mark Rose, 'Filling the Void—Verne, Wells and Lem', *Science Fiction Studies*, Vol. 8 (1981), p. 130.
11. P.K. Krishnamoorthy, *A. Scholar's Guide to Modern American Science Fiction* (Hyderabad: American Studies Research Centre, 1983), p. 20.
12. Patrick Parrinder, *Science Fiction: Its Criticism and Teaching* (London: Methuen and Co., 1982), p. 84.
13. Mark Hillegas, *op. cit.*, p. 24.
14. H.G. Wells, *The Outline of History* (1920 rpt. London: Cassell and Company Ltd., 1937), p. 1048.
15. *Ibid.*, pp. 1041-42
16. *Ibid.*, p. 1041.
17. H.G. Wells, Preface to *The World Set Free* (London: Collins Clear-Tyre Press, 1970), p. 21. (other quotations from the preface of the fiction are taken from this edition, and are indicated by page number/numbers in parentheses).
18. Quoted from Geoffery West, *H.G.Wells* (London: Gerald Howe, 1930), p. 199.
19. H.G. Wells, *op. cit.*, pp. 131-32.
20. Frederick A. Kreuziger, *Apocalypse And Science Fiction* (Chicago: Scholars Press, 1982), p. 106.
21. H.G. Wells, *op. cit.*, p. 22.

Olaf Stapledon and Aldous Huxley

3

I

This chapter deals with the two major British SF writers, Olaf Stapledon and Aldous Huxley. The First World War has given rise to the Utopia dreams concerning scientific progress and the dystopian nightmare concerning the world order. In the post World War I, Eugenics received a momentum and Pavlov's researches on conditioning offered a challenge to human society. In 1920s and 1930s Europe has witnessed the rise and the spread of Fascism in Italy, and Nazism in Germany. The Time Traveller of Sydney Fowler Wright's *The World Below* (1929) shows that catastrophic forces sweep out a civilization when it rises to its peak. Old forms of life disappear and new forms take their places in a never-ending cycle. Robert Herrick's *Sometime* (1933) is combination of utopia and satire. It begins as utopia, established chiefly as a point of view for satiric comment upon the modern world. In the future world, the old Xian Civilization collapses due to the series of wars and a new world with eugenic control of population, automatic machines, the World-State, is developed. In this world-order, the concept of parenthood has changed. Parenthood is not a matter of individual choice: mating is possible only after obtaining prior religious sanction of approval. This new world has dystopian suggestions. In R.C. Sherriff's *The Hopkins Manuscript* (1939) men face a cosmic disaster with orderly courage, but they fail to cope with the man-made disaster, such as war, which destroys everything. Sidney used fantasy mode for the creation of cyclic worlds; Harrick for utopian world with dystopian suggestions; and Sherriff for the catastrophic world. No doubt, these writers have contributed to British SF in the post-World War I, but the most notable SF writers are Olaf Stapledon and Aldous Huxley.

Less skilled as a story teller than Wells, Staplendon is broader in his cosmic sweep in fantasy. His SF deals not only with different human species but also with new space-time revealed in the twentieth-century mathematics and astronomy. He employs fantasy mode to enlarge the horizon of British SF, and attributes a deeper philosophical meaning to it. Besides Stapledon, in the post-World War I period, Aldous Huxley, the grandson of H.G. Wells's biology teacher, Thomos Huxley, is also an important writer in so far as he enlarged the horizon of British SF in his own way. Huxley, the main stream novelist, turned to write SF because he thought that SF is an important *genre* which caters to the needs of the technological era. His SF is imbued with a philosophical meaning though we miss in it Stapledon's cosmic sweep in fantasy. He uses fantasy as an effective mode and creates the nightmare of the future technocratic era. As such, an attempt has been made here to explore relation between fantasy and reality in Stapledon's *Last and First Men* (1930), *Star Maker* (1937) and Huxley's *Brave New World* (1932), *Apes and Essence* (1939).

II

Stapledon, *Last and First Men* (1930) is a saga of humanity stretching from the present time to two billion years, covering the entire solar system. The human race rises, flourishes, and falls eighteen times, encountering conflicts among nations, natural calamities, alien opposition and results of their own inadequacies. As he has cited in his preface to *Last and First Men,* he has tried "to invert a story which may seem a possible, or at least not wholly impossible, account of the future of man," and "to make that story relevant to the change that is taking place today in man's outlook (p. v.)." Stapledon makes fantasy about the future of man acceptable to readers by providing a rational ground to his fantastic hypothesis. The conflicts among nations drive human race to the verge of extinction, and in the brutal struggle for existence, human species adapts itself to environment and forms new species which drift from one planet to other for survival. This fantastic hypothesis is based on the theories of evolution, especially by Charles Darwin and Lamark. Darwin in *Origin of Species* (1859) points at the inevitability of evolutionary change in a world in which each species tends to produce more individuals than can find a place provided that "there is sufficient variability, at least part of which is transmissible to the next generation, to give material for a natural selection within and between the species, comparable with the artificial selection practised by animal and plant breeders."[1] Besides Darwin's therory of evolution, Lamark also proposed the theory of adaption of living beings to environment, and, according to him, new needs arise in animals as a result of change in the environment. This leads to new types of behaviour involving new uses of pre-existing organs. Their use leads to an increase in size or to other methods of functioning. Conversely, the disuse of other parts leads to their decline. Consequently, the resulting material alternatives are inherited.[2] Once this hypothesis is accepted, Stapledon invents the unfamiliar world with familiar places, human features and human reactions to make the fantasy acceptable to readers. He imagines of conflicts among the Balkan countries, America and China; the Anglo-French War, the Russia-German War, and the failure of League of Nations after World War I, leading to the disaster which drifts human race to the threshold of extinction. But some human beings survive and evolve into the Eighteen Men through the successive stages. The most distinctive feature of the Third Men is their great lean hands. The fantastic beings, the Fifth Men, the Great Brains which are evolved after expirements in selective breeding, manipulation of the hereditary factors in germ cells, the fertilized ovum and the growing body, bear human characteristics. A member of the eighteenth species of men, living in the extremely distant future (who is the narrator of the story) talks of the features of the Fifth Men giving precise details:

> By inhibiting the growth of the embryo's body, and the lower organs of the brain itself, and at the same time greatly stimulating the growth of the cerebral hemispheres, the dauntless experiments succeeded at last in creating an organism which consisted of a brain twelve feet across, and a body most of which was reduced to a mere vestige upon the under-surface of the brain. The only parts of the body which were allowed to attain the natural size were the arms and hands....

> The sensory equipment of this trunkless brain was a blend of the natural and artificial. The optic nerves were induced to grow out along two flexible probosces, five feet long, each of which bore a huge eye at end.... Scent and taste were developed as a chemical sense, which could distinguish almost all compounds and elements by their flavour.[3]

Besides human features of the Fifth Men, the authenticity of human reactions to the events contributes to the credibility to the content of fantasy. After the first dark age, twenty-eight men and seven women are left. There has been a world wide disaster and they themselves have been saved only by their remoteness and the Arctic ice from a fate that has overwhelmed all their fellow-men. They think that at whatever cost of toil and misery they must people the earth again. In generous minds a common purpose and common suffering breed a deep passion of comradeship. These, in their loneliness and their sense of obligation, experience not only comradeship, but a vivid communion with one another as instruments of a sacred cause. The Fifth Men are faced with a grave moral problem that "what right had man to interface in a world already possessed by beings who were obviously intelligent, even though their mental life was incomprehensible to man?" The natives on Venus determine to destroy themselves in the process. Titanic explosion are engineered, which cause the invaders serious damage, and electrolysis pours more and more free oxygen into the atmosphere. This dissolved oxygen in the ocean water has a disastrous effect upon the oceanic organisms. The narrator says: "The horror of the slaughter produced a haunting guiltiness in all men's minds, an unreasoning disgust with humanity for having been driven to murder in order to save itself"(221). The Last Men face the dire consequences of the cooling of the sun. Their human spirit still persists and they imagine with courage and hope that "If any of this human seed should fall upon good ground, it will embark, we hope, upon a semewhat rapid biological evolution and produce in due season whatever complex organic forms are possible in its environment" (278).

The conflicts among nations during the first four years of the twentieth century culminated into World War I (1914-18).

Germany and Austria struck at France and Russia and Serbia; the German armies marched towards Belgium, Britain immediately came into the war on the side of Belgium, bringing in Japan, as her ally, and very soon Turkey followed on the German side. Italy entered the war against Austria in 1915, and Bulgaria joined the Central Powers in the October of that year. In 1916 Rumania and in 1917 the United States and China were forced into war against Germany.[4] As German armies passed from victory to victory, Germany's bid for world dominion becomes clearer and sharper. The Allies at bay turned to America as the one hopes for making the world "safe for democracy." This appeal did not fall on deaf ears. America felt within herself the stirring of her future mission as the world champion of democracy. America entered the war on the side of the Allies whatever, in the hope of making every effort to establish a new world order based on freedom and security.[5] By 1918, mostly Europe was in a grip of fourth year, the whole world was suffering from the shortage of clothing and housing. Business and economic life were profoundly disorganised. Everyone was worried and most of the people were leading a life of unwanted discomfort.[6] League of Nations was formed after World War I to minimise the differences among nations but its taxing conditions sowed the seeds of World War II. Stapledon was not happy with these contemporary trends. During World War I, he served three years with the Friends' Ambulance Unit, attached to the French Armed Forces. It is that war and its aftermatch which haunted him rather than the Civil War in Spain.[7] He individuates his sense of dissatisfaction in the form of fantasy about the future human race. He applies the principles of evolution, proposed by Darwin and Lamark, to rise and fall of civilizations. Oswald Spengler coined his theory of cyclic history after World War I, in which he posed the problem of progress and regress of civilizations.[8] Taking cue from the principles of evolution and Spenglerian theory of cyclic history, he creates the vivid and unfamiliar picture of the human race on the cosmic level. Towards that end he employs the fantastic hypothesis as a take off point to create the 'other world.'

Last and First Men deals with a cyclic history of the human race covering the time span from the present to the extinction of the eighteenth and the last species of men on the planet Neptune, some 2,000,000,000 years in the future. One of the Last Men succeeds in transmitting to his distant ancestors the incredible saga of a history that is our future. In the century after the World War (1914-1918), there was a brief tragic conflict between France and England which was brought about due to some basic conflicts of temperament. This conflict persisted creating tensions although none of them wanted war. During this period, in both the countries everything seemed completely disorganized. Famine, riot, looting and above all the rapidly accelerating and quite uncontrollable spread of disease, distintegrated both the states, and brought war to a standstill. The management of each country was taken over, for a brief period, by the League of Nations. With the eclipse of France and England, Europe was led by Germany. The Germans, for their part, were aggrieved because Americans had ousted them from the most profitable field of enterprise, as also from the exploitation of Russian Asiatic oil. America, having used up most of her own supplies, was now anxious to complete with the still prolific sources under the Chinese control, by forestalling Germany in Russia. Individuals who thought of themselves as wholehearted Europeans, feared that at any moment they might succumb to same ridiculous epidemic of patriotism, and participate in the further crippling of Europe. This dread was one cause of the formation of a European Confederacy. Obstensibly the motive of this act was peace, but America interpreted it as directed against herself, and withdrew from the League of Nations. China, the 'natural enemy' of America, remained within the League, hoping to use it against her rival. A chinese physicist invented a method for the disintegration of the atom. It blasted a fleet of American plane coming to invade Europe. America attacked with poison gas and left Europe a wasteland. Asia united under China, and the two rival cultures ruled over the world: American wealth, power and activity, and Chinese pessimism, nostalgia, and passivity. When dichotomy culminated into war, it caused heavy destruction:

> In England, however, there were no schools, and no population; for early in the war, and American air-base had been established in Ireland, and England had been repeatedly devastated. At the other side of the world, the Japanese Islands had been similarly devastated in the vain American effort to establish there an air-base from which to reach the heart of the enemy. So far, however, neither China nor America had been seriously damaged; but recently the American biologists had devised a new malignant germ, more infectious and irresistible than anything hitherto known. Its work was to disintegrate the highest levels of the nervous system, and therefore to render all who were even slightly affected incapable of intelligent action; while a severe attack caused paralysis and finally death. With this weapon the American military had already turned one Chinese city into a bedlam; and wandering bacilli had got into the brains of several high officials throughout the province, rendering their behaviour incoherent. It was becoming the fashion to attribute allone's blunders to a touch of the new microbe. Hitherto no effective means of resisting the spread of this plague had been discovered (54).

In the scientific and technological era, a war is fought with a new malignant germ besides nuclear weapons. A nature of war is changed and its effects are more gruesome. In the year 2400, the World State is formed with an American President and a Chinese vice-president. Till 4000, the world is Americanized under a World Financial Directorate. In the Utopian world, the continents are artificialized. Sahara is a lake-district of sun-proud resorts; the arctic regions are armed by directed ocean currents. Man's normal life-span is two centuries; his amusements are the dance of the aeroplanes. The collapse of the first world civilization was due to the sudden failure of the supplies of coal and oil. Bacterial war is out-broken, and with it the ancient 'American madness', which long ago has been used against China, then devastated America. The great stations of water-power and wind-power are wrecked by lunatic mobs. The whole population vanishes in an orgy of cannibalism.To this extent, Stapledon extrapolates contemporary tendencies into fantasy. He has to assert that scientific progress makes modern war mechanised and fatal, and the modern war intensifies horror and brutality. He also reiterates that conflicts among nations on the earth lead to that kind of disaster which poses a threat of extinction for the humanity as a whole. After narrating the brutal consequences of the mechanised wår, Stapledon creates purely imaginary world of rise and fall of human species in the cyclical form, and *Last and First Men* ceases to be fantasy. It becomes an imaginary account of the rise and fall of the eighteen human species. Civilization rises again in Pantagonia; water-power develops and science re-discovers how to break up the atom for power. A serious clash between the two classes destroys Pantagonia. The rediscovery of atomic energy causes the downfall of the Pantagonia civilization in a chain explosion. Only twenty-eight men and seven women remain alive in a region near the North Pole. In the ten million years that ensued, the monkeys rise as a competitive, intelligent race, commanding subhuman slaves. The Martians invade the earth and they come as a cloud. The new type of life on Mars takes shape from another of these subvital kinds of molecular organization. Men fight Martians with artifical lightening for three hundred thousand years and before the Martian depart men are turned into children belonging to some dark age of thirty million years. Then the Third Men appear in the wilderness and then civilization rises utilizing wind, water, tidal power and the earth's internal heat. They develop manipulative skills, especially in biology, manipulating even foetus and the germ-plasm. Finally, they create the Fourth Men, the Great Brains. The Great Brains conduct researches which determines perfect man. They create two identical twins of opposite sexes which are produced from a single fertilized ovum: Adam and Eve of a new and glorious human species, the Fifth Men. They develop art, science, and philosophy. They are confronted with the most unexpected physical crisis, and fear that the collision of the moon and the earth will cause destruction. It causes migration of the Fifth Men to Venus. There, the contemporary intelligent life forms are destroyed, the planet is reshaped. Under the attack of bacteria on Venus, the Fifth Men sink into a dark age. The Sixth Men appear, after some millions of years; they were seal-like amphibians. The Seventh Men, who develop from the

Fifth along with the Sixth, are pigmies organised for flight through the air. The sun absorbs the nebula and doubles in size; Neptune becomes torried except at the poles. During a long sojourn on Neptune, ten species of men are formed one after another. At last, the Eighteenth Men appear, with occipital eyes in addition to an astronomical eye on the crown of the head. At intervals, the Last Men think as a racial unit. They even move backward in time to experience the life of the past. The cyclical history of rise and fall of human civilization does not embody the contemporary tendencies in society. It does not concern with reality in the present society but a different kind of reality. The Last Men experience the vastness of cosmos and minuteness of man: "the whole duration of humanity, with its many sequent species and its incessant downpour of generations, is but a flash in the life of the cosmos. Spatially, also man is inconceivably minute"(239). The Last Man philosophically expresses the nature and future of cosmos:

> Within this spatio-temporal sphere of ours we remark what we call the Beginning and what we call the End. In the Beginning there came into existence, we know not how, that all pervading and unimaginably tenuous gas which was the parent of all material and spiritual existence within time's known span. It was in fact a very multitudinous yet precisely numbered host. From the crowding together of this great population into many swarms, arose in time the nebulate, each of which in its turn condenses as a galaxy universe of stars. The stars have their beginnings and their ends; and for a few moments somewhere in between their beginnings and their ends a few, very few, may support mind. But in due course will come the Universal End, when all the wreckage of the galaxies will have drifted together as a single, barren, and seemingly changeless ash, in the midst of a chaos of unavailing energy" (267).

The Last Man comes to know that "there are many universes too remote to be estimated." According to Mark Hilleges, Stapledon presents a ghastly materialistic philosophy that there is no heaven or hell, that when a man dies he is gone for ever, and that the only hope man can have is to improve his lot through the application of science.[9] Stapledon reflects on man's place in the universe and puts forth the view that man is like a tiny speck in the vast cosmos whose existence is not altogether meaningless and that his worth lies in the human spirit engaged in the persistent struggle for human survival. In the fiction the eighteen species rise and fall in the cyclic form. Stapledon's understanding of reality is that human life exists in the cyclical way. An idea of the cyclical human life is not new to Hindu view of life. But Stapledon views it from a different standpoint. From his point of view the important issue is 'Which is the centre of cosmos?' On the basis of the rise and fall of human species for the eighteen times, his approach to reality is that cosmos is without divine centre.

Last and First Men is especially concerned with rise and fall of the human species for eighteen times. After the fall of Last Men, Stapledon is optimistic about the spread of humankind in future. In it events relating to rise and fall of human species follow cause and effect relationship. The fall of one species leads to the rise of other. The environmental factors and scientific progress shape the course of human species. Logic and inner consistency make the fiction acceptable to readers. Usually fantasy is opposed to reason but in *Last and First Men,* it is not opposed to reason. What may at first sight seems to be paradox lies in the heart of fantasy in SF. In that world what he relates consistently is true and it accords with the laws of that world and reader believes in it. The fiction covers the period of the two billion years. Action in the story takes place on the different planets in the solar system and it attributes cosmic dimension to SF. The characteristics like wide time-span, cosmic dimension and many characters assign epic dimension to SF. Epic grandeur arises from cosmic dimension and wide time-span. To Chad Walsh, "*Last and First Men* is a magnificent prose epic of what evolution might do with two billion years; it shows us giganatic brains based in ferroconcrete buildings and the admirable 'eighteenth man' a species gifted with telepathy and a high level group mind."[10]

In Stapledon's case, he treats the basic assumption as a take off point and creates imaginary world which has no close link with the present world. His main concern is to create vivid picture of cyclical history of rise and fall of civilization. At this juncture, it becomes important to ask, is fantasy myth? Mircea Eliade constructs a definition for myth that embraces various and complementary viewpoints:

> Myth narrates a sacred history; it relates an event that took place in a primordial Time, the fabled time of the 'beginnings.' In other words, myth tells how, through the deeds of Supernatural beings, a reality came into existence, be it the whole of reality, the cosmos, or only a fragment of reality.... Myth then, is always an accout of a 'creation' it relates how something was produced began to be. Myth tells only of that which really happened, which manifested itself completely.... In short, myths describe the various and sometimes dramatic breakthrough of the sacred (or the 'supernatural') into the world.[11]

Last and First Men does not narrate sacred history. Secondly, it does not state how, through the deeds of Supernatural beings, a factual world came into existence. But it deals with the creation of order in the forms of different living species after the disorder in the present world. In fantasy, when the human species remain on the verge of extinction, some human species survive and then cyclically eighteen species are created. Stapledon imaginatively conceives restoration of order after the phase of disorder. Stapledon has aptly said in the Preface "some readers, taking my story to be the attempt at prophecy, may deem it unwarrantly pessimistic. But it is not prophecy, it is myth, or an essay in myth" (p. vi). *Last and First Men* is an imaginary tale of human predicament having the potential of myth.

III

As it has been pointed out earlier, Stapledon is unhappy with the warring nations in the First World War (1914-1918), and imagines that all efforts to patch up differences are turned futile. In the preface to *Star Maker* he writes:

> At a moment when Europe is in danger of a catastrophe worse that of 1914...year by year, month by month, the plight of our fragmentary and precarious civilization becomes more serious. Fascism abroad grows more bold and ruthless in its foreign ventures, more tyrannical towards its own citizens, more barbarian in its contempt for life of the mind. Even in

> our country we have reason to fear a tendency toward militarization and curtailment of civil liberty. Moreover, while the decades pass, no resolute step is taken to alleviate the injustice of our social order. Our outworn economic system dooms millions to frustration.[12]

In this passage, he highlights a tendency toward militarization and curtailment of civil liberty, prevalent in the post-World War I period. He feels discontented because no firm steps are taken to alleviate the injustice of social order. In *Star Maker* (1937), he uses the overwrought and often misunderstood words like 'spiritual' and 'worship', to suggest an experience which "involves detachment from all private, all social, all racial ends; not in the sense that it leads a man to reject them, but it makes to prize them in a new way"(9). His faith in capitalism and parlimentary democracy dwindles; he sees and experiences the mingling of hope and despair in the face of future. He feels convinced that the Judeo-Christian God is as dead as the churches where the hypocritical bourgeoisie gather to invoke His blessings on their profit-making and their imperialist wars.[13] Taking cue from a tendency towards militarization and curtailment of civil liberty, and loss of faith in religion in the technocratic society, he constructs the story of space-voyage, having cosmic dimension. According to P.S. Krishnamoorthy, *Star Maker* presents:

> An odyssey of the spirit which finds everything else before it finds itself. The fiery brilliance of imaginations and the dizzying variety of invention make the work a true classic of science fiction.[14]

Star Maker is certainly an unusual SF, the basic pattern of which is old and familiar i.e., to make travels to other places, a unifying and central metaphor. Here the imaginary journey becomes a metaphor for the inner quest to know the universe.

Star Maker is a sequel to *Last and First Men*. Its theme, however, is not merely the story of Man, but the story of Life and Mind in the Cosmos through all times. To J.O. Bailey, it seeks to offer "explanation for the mystery of life and space-time as the explanation may be surmised from biology, astronomy, and mathematics."[15] A narrator, an Englishman, walks into an open field and looks upward at the stars and fantasies about his space travel. A traveller's purpose of undertaking this journey into space is not merely to observe the universe in a disinterested fashion, but to effect some kind of mental and spiritual traffic with other worlds through mutual enrichment and fellow-feeling. He finds the 'Other World' which seems similar to the world on the earth. Bvalltu, the philosopher invites the narrator to accept the hospitality of his mind. Civilization has reached a stage of growth much like that which is familiar to a traveller. Industrialism is already far advanced in many countries. Exploitation of workers by capitalists, in the industrialised era, and machines create social and economical disorders. The relationships between the wealthy and the official, and pariahs and half pariahs are like the master and slave relationship between Eloi and Morlocks in *The Time Machine.* In *The Time Machine,* Wells imagines the future implication of the class conflicts in the present society. Stapledon does not stress seriously the contemporary problem in fantasy. His main concern is his vision.

The sustaining motive of the pilgrimage of the narrator and Bvalltu have been the hunger which formely drove men on the Earth in search of God. The narrator says:

> ...the spirit which we all in our hearts obscurely knew and haltingly prized, the spirit which on Earth we sometimes call humane, was Lord of the Universe, or outlaw; almighty, or crucified. And now it was becoming clear to us that if the cosmos had any lord at all, he was not that spirit but some other, whose purpose in creating the endless fountain of worlds was not fatherly towards the beings that he had made, but alien, inhuman, dark (99).

They think that the cosmic spirit is not friendly, sympathetic, but alien, inhuman and dark. Here Stapledon reacts against the father-image of creator of cosmos. They visit different planets. On the very small but earthlike planet, they discover a quasi-human race which is probably unique. A very different and fairly common quasi-human kind is sometimes produced by planets rather larger than the Earth. That quasi-human kind is developed "from a sort of five-pronged marine animal rather like a star fish." The basic pattern of minds of Human echinoderms is like our own. Each individual is capable of budding a new individual, and only after stimulation by a kind of pollen emanating from the whole tribe. The grains of this ultra-miscroscopic fine pollen dust are not germ-cells but 'genes.' Every child is fathered by the tribe as a whole. The greatest religion of this strange world is not religion of love but religion of self. In that world, modern industrial civilization introduces artifical 'super-tribes' and they exercise absolute power over all individual minds. In democratic countries, women have attained greater economic independence, and their demand for fertilization by 'boute-men' causes the whole matter to be commercialized. In non-democratic countries, a tyrant is the god-sent hero. In some lands artificial insemination is carried out in all countries to alter the composition of the whole quasi-human race. Henceforth civilization decays and the race enters into a sort of civilized barbarism, which, in essence, is sub-human and incapable of change. At last the race is destroyed by the ravages of a small rat-like animal against which it can devise no protection. On certain very large and aqueous planets, they find that civilization has been achieved by marine organisms. A traveller narrates:

> One of them a mollusc-like creature, living in the coastal small ows, acquired a propensity to drift in its boat like shell on the sea's surface thus keeping in touch with its drifting vegetable fond. As the ages passed, its shell become adapted to navigation. Mere drifting was supplemented by means of a crude sail, a membrane extending from the creature's back (90).

Morphological and physiological changes in Mantiloids pertain to a new mode of navigational life. One of these becomes the intelligent master of that great world. Stapledon presents human situation in the society of Nautiloids in which masters are different from the workers. Masters are on the whole more prudent, far seeking, independent, self-reliant; workers are more impetuous, more ready to sacrifice themselves in a social cause. When a traveller and Bvalltu visit the world of Nautiloids, a desperate struggle is being waged among masters and workers. Very rapidly the material fabric of civilization ends into pieces.

A traveller describes a symbiotic race on certain large planets, much hotter than our tropics. Of these worlds, one, an immense and very aqueous sphere, "produced in time a dominant race which was not a single species but an intimate symbiotic parternership of two very alien creatures. The one comes of a fish-like stock. The other was in appearance something like crustacean" (104). There is mutual co-operation between two species, the fish-like creatures, Ichthyoids, and the crab-like or spider-like, 'crustaceans' or 'archanoids'. On the whole, the archanoids partners dominate in manual skill, experimental science, the plastic arts, and practical social organization. The ichthyoid partners excell in theatrical work, in literary arts, in the surprisingly developed music of that submarine world, and in the more mystical kind of religion.

Another world exhibits composite beings, avian creatures like sparrows that act with a flock-mind in a telepathy of 'radio' waves that amount to be a single centre of consciousness. They come across the other types of composite individuals, insect-like creatures. Civilization has turned the old disorderly towns into carefully planned subterranean cities; old irrigation channels into a widespread mesh of waterways for the transport of freight from district to district. It has introduced mechanical power and metals from outcrops and alluvial deposits. In a surprisingly short time that world becomes a federation whose members are distinct species. The narrator says "with sadness I realized that on the Earth, though all civilized beings belong to one and some biological species, such a happy issue of strife is impossible, simply because the capacity for community in the individual mind is still too weak" (121). Here Stapledon poses the situation contrasting to that on the earth, and satirises the lack of co-operation on the earth. On certain small planets, every organism on those planets, is at once an animal and a vegetable. Those organisms are planet-men, rooted vegetables or trees by day, but active animals by night, roaming sometimes far from the detached roots. Artificial photosynthesis, though, it can keep the body vigorous, fails to produce some essential vitamins. A disease of robotism, spreads throughout the population. Some worlds discover how to change the orbit of a planet by firing sub-atomic rockets. Some worlds, set out to colonize space end by attacking other worlds. Highly advanced worlds resist the other rival worlds with telepathic pressure. At the end of the wars, the symbiotics spread from world to world, and they create their own worlds, hollow globes of concentric spheres enclosing air around the ocean at the centre of the globe. Stapledon's apprehension of reality is that conflicts in human society pose a serious threat to wipe out human civilization if remedial measures are not implemented to abolish conflicts. To him, the earth is small in comparison to vast range of cosmos. Human beings are not only the living beings in cosmos and other planets too are inhibited by living beings.

Besides these aspects of reality, Stapledon attempts to answer the questions: Has cosmos a divine centre? Is cosmos expanding? Following the Utopian condition, inhabitants develop a single consciousness by telepathic means to interlock galaxy. Each conscious individual experience was sensory impressions of all the races in a system of worlds. The 'I' which represents the consciousness of the narrator expands to encompass the cosmic mind—all the 'I's of all minds and then seeks to know the Starmaker, the Creater. The narrator observes that the outer and middle layers of a mature star apparently consists of 'tissues' woven of currents of incandescent gases. These gaseous tissues live and maintain the Steller consciousness by intercepting part of the immense food of energy that is supplied from the congested and furiously active interior of the star. The innermost of the vital layers must be a kind of digestive apparatus which transmutes the crude radiations into forms required for the maintenance of the star's life. Outside that digestive area lies some sort of co-ordinating layer, which may be throughout of as the star's brain. The outer-most layers, including the corona, respond to the excessively faint stimuli of the star's cosmical environment, to light from the neighbouring stars, to cosmic rays, to the impact of meteors, to tidal stresses caused by the gravitational influence of planets or other stars. The life of the individual star is not restricted to physical movement; it is also, undoubtedly in some sense, a cultural and spiritual life. Most suprisingly, the physical nature of a star at any stage of its growth is in part an expression of the telepathic influence of other stars. To describe the mentality of stars is to describe unintelligible by means of intelligible. The narrator states, "I shall press on, which all my peers throughout the cosmos, to crown the cosmos with perfect and joyful insight, and to salute the Maker of Galaxies and Stars and Worlds with fitting praise" (209). He watches the birth of cosmos:

> Absolute spirit, self-limited for creativity, objectified from itself an atom of its infinite potentiality.
>
> This microcosm was pregnent with the germ of a proper time and space, and all kinds of cosmical beings.
>
> Within this punctual cosmos the myriad but not unnumbered physical centres of power, which men conceive vaguely as electrons, protons, and the rest, were first coincident with one another. And they were dormant. The matter of ten million galaxies lays dormant in a point.
>
> Then the Star Maker said, 'Let there be light.' And there was light.
>
> From all the coincident and punctual centres of power, light leapt and blazed. The cosmos exploded, actualizing its potentiality of space and time. The centres of power, like fragments of a bursting bomb were hurled apart. But each one retained in itself as a memory and a longing, the single spirit of the whole; and each mirrored in itself aspects of all others throughout all the cosmical space and time.
>
> No larger punctual, the cosmos now a volume of inconceivably dense matter and inconceivably expanding. And it was a sleeping and infinitely dissociated spirit.
>
> But so say that cosmos was expanding is equally to say that its members were contracting. The ultimate centres of power, each at first coincident with the punctual cosmos, themselves generated the cosmical space by their disengagement from each other. The expansions of the whole cosmos was but the shrinkage of all its physical units and of the wavelengths of its light (225).

Though the cosmos is ever of finite bulk, in relation to its minutiae of light-waves, it is boundless and centre-less. As the surface of a swelling sphere lacks boundary and centre, so the swelling volume of the cosmos is boundless and centre-less. The congested and exploding cloud of fire swells till it is of a planet's size, a star's size, size of whole galaxy, and of ten million galaxies. And in swelling thus it becomes more tenuous, less brilliant, less turbulent. In his imaginative vision, the narrator, in a view, cold and penetrating light, watches all the lives of stars and worlds, and of the galactic communities, and of myself, wherein then he stands confronted by "the infinity that men call God, and conceive according to their human cravings" (226). He sees nowhere in cosmical space, the *Star Maker,* the blazing source of the hypercosmical light, a sun more powerful than all suns together. His dream declares: "the Star Maker is perfect and absolute." In the typically irrational manner of dreams, that dream-myth which arises in his mind represents "the eternal spirit as beings at once the cause and the result of the infinite host of finite existence" (235). Patrick A. McCarthy has observed in *Science Fiction Studies* that Stapledon is free to make the *Star Maker* into "a figure that is neither good nor evil, neither God nor Satan but simply the narrator's conception of the creative force behind the growth of spirit in the cosmos."[17] In *Star Maker*, Stapledon creates the myth of creation of cosmos. He reacts against the Biblical myth of creation of cosmos by God, and deems Star Maker as a creative force behind cosmos. He reacts a new myth to cater to the need of technological era which demands new myth. He uses fantasy mode to create a myth. To Eric Rubkin and Robert Scholes, "Star Maker is a supreme attempt to use the art of science fiction to construct an imaginative sketch of the dread but vital whole of beings."[18]

In an attempt to give an explantation of what may happen in future world, he reconstructs the elements of story on the mythical line. His realization is that cosmos is without any divine centre and its creator is neither good nor evil. Stapledon's concept of reality is different than that of Wells. To Stapledon, reality is what he constructs. Wells seems to approach reality from outside whereas Stapledon's concept is different. He is moreover concerned with his inner reality; his vision.

IV

In the post-World War I period, besides Stapledon, Aldous Huxley is a significant SF writer who has given a dystopian turn to the British SF. Huxley's *Brave New World* (1932) is the most significant dystopian fiction in the twentieth century, with the possible exception of George Orwell's *Nineteen Eighty-Four* (1949) in British SF. The basic hypothesis in the fiction is that a desired human being is manufactured if ovum from female and spermatozoon from male are fertilized artificially to form an egg; an embryo is predestined and a baby is conditioned. Once the basic assumption is accepted by readers, Huxley creates the dystopian world of future technocratic society. He invests unfamiliar future world with familiar, minute, precise and human details. The various Bureaux of propaganda and the College of Emotional Engineering are housed in sixty-storey building in Fleet Street. In the basement and on the lower floors are the presses and offices of the three great London newspapers. Then come the Bureaux of propaganda by Television. Above are the research laboratories. 'Bokanovsky's process' and the biochemical treatment of embryos are described with proliferation, divison, and from a single egg ninety-six beings are formed. Bokanovskification consists of a series of arrests of development and it checks the normal growth and paradoxically enough, the egg responds by budding. Podsnap's Technique immensely accelerates the process of ripening. Extract of carpus Luteum is injected in embryos; doses of pituitary are administered. The artificial material is installed on every bottle at 112 meters. The massive doses of beg's stomach extract is given to avoid anaemia of embryo. Sex tests are carried out in the neighbourhood of 200 meters. Intellectual conditioning is done after the foetuses have lost their tails. Due to the human features, the fantastic beings, Alpha, Beta, Gamma, Delta, Semi-morons, Epsilons, and the Savage, appear real. The Director, the controller, Helmholtz Watson, Bernard, Henry Forster, Lenina are Alpha who regulate the working in the centre. Bernard is Alpha-plus psychologist, and Mustapha Mond is the controller. The warden is Alpha-minus, "short, red moon-faced, and broad-shouldered, with a loud booming voice, very well adapted to the utterence of hypnopaedic wisdom."[19] Helmholtz Watson is a lecturer at the college of Emotional Engineering, "a powerfully built man, deep-chested, broad-shouldered, massive, and yet quick in his movements, springy and agile. The round strong pillar of his neck supported, beautifully shaped head. His head was dark and curly, his features strongly marked (78). Besides human features human reactions of the characters provide authenticity to this imaginative creation. In the visit of Henry and Lenina to Westminster, Henry says "Every one works for everyone else. We cann't do without anyone. Even Epsilons are useful. We couldn't do without Epsilons." She is glad that he is not Epsilons. She is shocked due to Henry's words, and her shock is stained with fear and surprise. When Lenina and Bernard enter the puelbo of Malpais, she sees an almost naked Indian who is slowly climbing down the ladder from the first-floor terrace of a neighbouring house, with the tremendous caution of extreme old age. She experiences horror and amazement. Besides Lenina'a horror and amazement, Bernard's isolation, emptiness, agony are real. In Ford's day Celebration, participants sing, dance, drink, and wait for Ford. But Bernard does not involve himself in the activities. He finds himself isolated from the illusionary surrounding. The narrator says:

> He was as miserably isolated now as he had been when the service began—more isolated by reason of his unreplenished emptiness, his dead satiety. Separate and unatoned, while the others were being fused into the Greater Being; alone even in Morgana's embrace—much more alone, indeed, more helplessly himself than he had ever been in his life before. He had emerged from the crimson twilight into the common electric glare with a self-consciousness intesified to the pitch of agony (100).

Bernard is reluctant to participate in the merry-making. He is comparatively short in height and it is symbolic of his difference from those who are conditioned. Being different in his attitude to the other world, he experiences isolation, emptiness, agony and feels suffocated in that jubilant atmosphere. Huxley infuses unfamiliar world with precise, familiar and human details, and though future world remains unfamiliar, unknown and strange to readers, reactions and responses of characters are typically human.

During the decade begining with 1926 'conditioning' played a less conspicuous role in the text books but more attention was paid in laboratories. The word, 'conditioning' did not enter the popular vocabulary before the publication of Pavlov's research work in psychology.[20] The Russian psychologist, Ivan Pavlov in his experiment paired a bell with meat powder. A stimulus elicited salivation in dogs. After repeated presentations the dogs salivated to the bell.[21] In that period, in Animal Husbandary, expirements were performed to fertilize animals artificially. Considerable steps were taken in the domains of biological science and psychology. In the essay 'Progress: Now the Achievements of Civilization Will Eventually Bankrupt the Entire World' (1928), he writes:

> Uninheritable progress, due to tradition, has genuinely taken place in the realm of science and technology, where each worker stands on the shoulders of his predecessors. In the realm of morals, the refinement of traditional codes may lead to a certain ethical progress throughout a whole society. But the greater part of what is called moral progerss consists merely in changes that are entirely without ameliorative direction. Progress in the arts is very limited and as soon as the technique of artistic expression is perfected, ceases altogether to exist.[22]

Huxley is dissatisfied with the present state of technological progerss, which ignores the spiritual, ethical, aesthetic, cultural and religious values in human society. This dissatisfaction works as a stimulus and as a result of this he individuates his sense of dissatisfaction by creating a vivid picture of future technological society based on Stability, Community and Identity. Taking his cue from experiments in artificial fertilization and conditioning, he extrapolates these tendencies in future society.

The new world-order comes into being after the Nine years' War that begins in A.F. 141. In this new world, there is a choice between World Control and Stability on the one hand or barbarism on the other. The World Controllers are successful when they turn to ectogenesis, neo-pavlovian conditioning, hypnopaedia, and a campaign against the past. In the future society, ovum and spermatozoon are fertilized artificially, and 'Bokanovsky's process' is implemented to manufacture ninety-six identical twins at a time from a single egg, on a mass scale. 'Bokanovsky's process' is the major instrument of social stability. After decantation, embryos are predestined and conditioned. Epsilon embryos, for instance, destined for labour in the tropics, are put in hot tunnels alternated with cold. They are bred to thrive on heat. Babies destined to be workers are given books and flowers and then are electrically shocked. Hypnoapaedia through speakers under the children' pillows make Gammas glad that they do not have to work hard as Betas, and they are not stupid like deltas. In the future technocratic society, gonadal harmones transfusion of young blood, magnesium salts are used to keep people young. All the physiological stigma of old age has been abolished. Vibro-vaccum message, an electrolytics are common. Commenting upon the scientific progress in the fiction, John Timmerman says:

> The terror of Bokanovsky' process is commonplace in our genetic laboratories, and being commonplace it is no longer terrible. The counter-culture radicals of the 1960s had strawberry soma, except they called it LSD. Yet Huxley warns us what we stand in the unchecked path of Scientism, the worship of Scientific method as a god unto itself. Dystopian literature tells us what we are in danger of losing; and perhaps Huxley's novel tells us what we live already lost.[23]

In the future society, education is imparted to the conditioned offsprings by machines. Inside boxes, voices use to speak. Information is fed to them to root class consciousness in their minds. Erotic games are taught to boys and girls. The importance is not given to moral education. To the Director "Moral education, which ought never, in any circumstances to be rational." There is no sense of morality as such, and so Lenina has multiple sexual relationship; Linda does not mind to have sexual relationship with Pope. Sex is sterile and degraded. Shakespeare's plays are not taught because they are old for the

Directors and Controllers. The Christian texts are outdated because they are about the past things. Religious teachings are ignored and the decline in religious values is well mirrored in the Ford's Day Celebration. In the great auditorium, the dedicated soma tablets are placed in the centre of the dinner table. The loving cup of strawberry ice-cream soma is passed from hand to hand, with the words, "I drink to my annihilation." The second Hymn was sung:

> Come' Greater Being, social friend
> Annihilating Twelve ... in ...one!
> We long to die, for when we end
> Our larger life has but began (95).

Huley employes the words 'Greater Being,' 'Social Friends,' 'larger life' in satirical sense. Morgana Rothchild and Bernard utter "I drink to the immence of His Coming." Here coming is not coming of Christ; it is an illusion. The loving cup of soma is circulated and the third Solidarity Hymn is sung:

> Feel how the Greater Being come!
> Rejoice and, in rejoicing die!
> Melt in the music of the drums!
> For I am you and you are I (96).

In these lines, again death is highlighted, while rejoicing. There is longing to feel union of 'you' and 'I' due to the charged physical passion, and not due to spiritual illumination. The President Switches off the music and with the final note of the final stanza, there is absolute silence of stretched expectancy. Morgana Rothschild cries that she hears him. Sarojini Engles; Jim Bokanovsky yells; Clara Deterding screams. Bernard also jumps up and shouts that he hears him; he is coming. There is an illusion of coming of the Greater Being because nobody is coming in reality. In future society, religious feelings are substituted by feelings of people in the false trance induced by soma. Huxley satirises people illusion of the Greater Being. The dancer sings:

> Orgy – porgy, Ford and Fun
> Kiss the girls and make them One,
> Boys at one with girls at peace
> Orgy – porgy gives release (98).

Here the word 'one' has no connection with the oneness of the Divine Being.

The debate between Mustapha and the Savage unfolds how religious values are looked down in the technocratic society. Mustapha Mond believes that the mordern world is one of the numerous things in heaven and earth that philosophers do not dream about. He thinks that in the modern world, men can be independent of God as long as they are youthful and prosperous. Mustapha Mond expresses his view but the savage does not agree with him:

> But there aren't any losses for us to compensate; religious sentiment is superfluous. And why should we go hunting for a substitute for youthful desires, when youthful desires never fail?. A substitute for distractions, when we go on enjoying all the old fooleries to the very last? What need have we of repose when our minds and bodies continue to delight in activity? Of consolation, when we have soma? Of something immovable, when there is no God? 'No, I think there quite probably is one' 'Then why?....'
>
> Mustapha Mond checked him. 'But he manifests himself in different ways to different men. In pre-modern times he manifested himself as the being that's described in these books. Now....
>
> 'How does he manifest himself now?' asked the savage.
>
> 'Well, he manifested himself as an absence; as though he weren't there at all.'
>
> 'That's your fault.'
>
> 'Call it the fault of civilization God isn't compatible with machinary and scientific medicine and universal happiness. You must make your choice. Our civilization has chosen machinery and medicine and happiness. That's why I have to keep these books locked up in the safe. They're smut. People would be shocked if....'
>
> The savage interrupted him. 'But isn't it natural to feel there's a God?' (277-78).

Mustapha Mond thinks that people believe in God because they are conditioned to believe in God. In the technocratic civilization, religious values like self-denial, chastity are superfluous. Civilization has chosen machinery, medicine and happiness. Christianity is replaced by soma. The Savage is a staunch believer in God and religous values, and expresses his liking for poetry; insists on freedom, goodness and sin in human life. The Savage has his ideas on freedom, religion and happiness, and they do not fit in the framework of the technocratic society and so the attempts are made by the Director and the Controller to torture and humilate the Savage; to suppress the individual voice in him.

In the sphere of art in the future society, in the various Bureaux of propaganda, there are the padded rooms in which the Sound-track writers, Synthetic composers do their delicate work. In Westminster Abbey Cabaret, the latest Synthetic Music is played. Here the writer satirises artificiality in the process of creativity.

In fantasy, Huxley presents the horrifying face of future which is the culmination of the present tendencies in society. He satirises the future society on the tenets of progress in psychology, science and technolgoy, and consequently decline in the sphere of religion, art; degradation of sex. He creates the dystopian picture of the future society which is technocratic hell. Mark Hilleges has commented, "He was against utopia not only because it would mechanize human life but because it would give abundance and leisure to everyone, making these no longer the special privilege of people like himself."[24] His chief strategy is that the conditioned happiness in the future world cuts men off from deep experience, keep them away from being fully human. His worry is that when everybody in the future enjoys abundance and leisure, life won't be worth living for anybody. To Patrick Parrinder, "The debunking of utopia exemplified by Aldous Huxley's *Brave New World* (1932) remains the representative expression of twentieth century anxieties."[25] In fantasy, the Director and the Controller take step to suppress the individual voices of Bernard and the Savage. They do not allow the ideas of others, which contradict their motto of the World's State's Stability, Communtiy, Identity to operate. From this standpoint, Huxley's *Brave New World* foreshadows the totalitarian state controlled by Big Brother in George Orwell's

Nineteen Eighty-Four. The difference is that Huxley is more concerned with science and technology and Orwell with politics. Huxley's vision of reality is of that society which adheres strictly to science and technology, and neglects religion, art, degrades and destabilises itself. He warns human society which firmly believes in science and technology, as shaping forces to stabilise it, irrespective of religion and art. It works as a curative.

V

In the second half of the nineteenth century and the beginning of the twentieth century, notable steps have been taken to study micro-organisms like bacteria, fungi, and viruses. Robert Koch (1843-1910) introduced technical methods for obtaining different micro-organisms in pure culture and described bacterial agents responsible for tuberculosis and cholera. Pupils of Louis Pasteur and Koch discovered causative micro-organism of a whole range of different diseases. Agricultural studies revealed that soil fertility was essentially dependent on micro-organisms and plant pathology was illuminated by the discovery of pathogenic bacteria and viruses.[26] The large majority of fungi are saprophytes (living on dead remains) and they, with the bacteria are the great agents of decay in nature. Some fungi are poisonous which contain poisonous substance such as alkaloids which render them extremly dangerous when used as foods.[27] After 1930, and especially after the World War II, the new methods were developed for the isolation of viruses responsible for human diseases.[28] As it has been already substantiated while interpreting *Brave New World,* Huxley views the technological progress with suspicion. He is dissatisfied with the present state of technological progress, and his dissatisfaction works as a stimulus. As a result of which he individuates this sense of dissatisfaction by creating the vivid, horrifying picture of the post-catastrophe world after World War III. Taking his cue from the experiments in microbiology, he extrapolates the contemporary tendencies in the future society in *Ape and Essence* (1948).

Here the assumption is that the use of fungi, bacteria, viruses in war makes war-machinery more dreadful to cause heavy destruction. Bob Briggs, a screenplay writer, discovers an imaginary film script in a Hollywood dustbin, whose author William Tallies has set out to give a picture of California as it may be in 2108, after World War III, the 'thing'. The narrator expresses that after World War II, people amuse themselves with power politics and political unrest in the world; aggressive nationalism and imperialism emerge, and they culminate into World War III in which nuclear bombs are used, and bacteria-bearing aerosols and many species of virus carrying aphides and other insects are released in air. A New Zealand botanist, Dr. Alfred Poole, who joins an expedition for rediscovery of America is landed at E1 Segundo. Dr. Poole is captured in front to a ruined bunglow, by "three villainous-looking men, black-beared dirty and ragged." They are the wilder and backward people, the familiar descendants of the survivors of the great disaster, World War III, who live in the ruins of Los Angles. After arrest, Dr. Poole is carried to the graveyard, lying between the ferro-concrete towers of Hollywood and those of Wilshire Boulevard. In the graveyard, he sees four men and two young women, dressed identically in shirts and trousers of tattered homespun on which 'No' is written, are busy with shovels around on an open grave. 'No' signifies their reluctance to believe in good; to take into account aesthetic, cultural aspects of human society. The eldest grave digger takes out watch and jewellery from the corpse of the Director of Golden Rule Brewing Carporation whose business was heartening good during World War II. Suddenly the Chief whips the kneeling grave digger, and possess the handsome diamond ring. The Chief tells him that it is 'Democracy' and "the Law says that everything belongs to the proletariat...in other words, it all goes to the State"[29] For three generations the dwindling remnant of these who survive after the disastrous effects of the technological progress, live precariously in the wilderness. It is only during the last thirty years it has been safe for them to enjoy the buried remains.

In the post-catastrophe world, as a consequence of fungal, bacterial and viral warfare, low fertility is caused by erosion of soil; plants and animal are infected by fungi, bacteria and viruses; the problem of malnutrition is due to the acute shortage of food, and besides these, the human beings are suffered from glander, the disease which was once common in horses. There are communal ovens and in the furnace, books from public Library are baked to prepare breads. Dr. Poole is disgusted by the repelling spectacle. He tells the Chief about cultural and the social inheritance of humanity's painfully acquired wisdom. The Chief tells him that the people in the post-catastrophe world can not read. No books are published after the 'thing'. The future society is degraded, and he does not respect aesthetic and cultural aspects of human society.

As Ford Day celebration in *Brave New World,* Belial Day celebration in *Ape and Essence,* deploys the reversal of religious and ethical values. The people after World War III believe in Belial, the Devil. Belial is Almighty, and 'He' gets the control and wins the battle and takes possession of everybody. In the future world, the belief in God is substituted by belief in Belial. In the eyes of the Chief, "the chief end of Man is to propitiate Belial, deprecate His enmity and avoid destruction for as long as possible" (68). Church is the body of which Belial is the head and all possessed people are the members. On Belial Day, the 'purification of the Race' is carried out in the presence of Arch-Vicar, the incarnation of spiritual authority. The narrator expresses:

> Church and State,
> Greed and Hate
> Two baboon - persons
> In one Supreme Gorilla. (77)

Church is the controlling centre of the State as in the medieval time. Greed and hate are merged in one Supreme Gorilla, Belial. As Dr. P.S. Krishnamoorthy rightly points out, "*In Ape and Essence* (1948), Huxley describes a post-catastrophe world that has become medieval, with the Church as the dominant power. It is another sharp satire on humanity's failure to understand itself."[30] In the State, it is believed that children are born deformed because of their mothers, the "chosen vessel of unholiness." In fact, deformity in children is the effect of the radiation of the gamma-rays. Mothers who bear monsters are 'mockery of man.' Every mother of a monster is worked down, and their heads are shaven and the preliminary whipping is administrated. Belial is propitiated only by blood, and for that sake, deformed children are inhumanly killed, and a half a pint of blood is allowed to spill out on the Altar, and then tiny corpses are tossed mercilessly into the darkness. Dr. Poole is shuddered with the spine-chilling horror. The Dark Age has returned and in it religious values are perverted; religion is practicised in the inhuman way; people belive in evil, and not in good.

Huxley sees progerss and nationalism as the two fatal ideas which upset the equilibirium of Nature and rush upon his own ruin. Arch-Vicar asserts that from the begining of the industrial revolution Belial foresees that "man would be made so overwhelmingly bumptious by the mircle of their own technology that they would soon lose all sense of reality."[30] He says:

> Progress—the theory that you can get something for nothing; the theory that you can gain in one field without paying for your gain in another; the theory that you alone understand and meaning of history; the theory that you know what's going to happen fifty years from now; the theory that, in the teeth of all experience, you can foresee all the consequences of your present actions; the theory that Utopia lies just a head and that, since ideal ends justify the most abominable means, your privilege and duty to rob, swindle, torture; enslave and murder all those who, in your opinion (which is by definition, infalliable), abstruct the onward march to the earthy paradise...and there was Nationalism...the theory that the state you happen to be subject to is the only true god, and that all other states are false gods, that all these gods, true as well as false, have the mentality of juvenile deliquents; and that every conflict over prestige, power of money is a crusade for the Good, the True and the Beautiful. (93-94)

In the grab of scientists and politicians, Belial desires for the degradation and the destruction of the human race. As Harold L. Berger has viewed, "In the expressionistic cinematic scenarion, which comprises the major portion of *Ape and Essence*, Huxley dams a detached science serving as a prostitute of malevolent forces."[31] Huxley unrelentlessly condemns the moral indifference of the scientist, who works "only for Truth." Scientists and politicians are inspired "by an alien consciousness, a consciousness that willed their undoing and willed it more strongly than they were able to will their own happiness and survival" (96). If they have not been possessed, they have negotiated peace with victory, but they cannot. It is impossible for them "to act in their own self-interest." They dream of progress and nationalism but their dream is shattered in the forms of the disastrous consequences of World War III. Huxley has emphasised that modern man in the technological era has degraded himself religiously, ethically, aesthetically, culturally, and politically, and attained the level of ape, and his essence of man is lost. The narrator says:

> But man, proud man,
> Drest in a little briet authority...
> Most ignorant of what he is most assur'd
> His glassy essence...like an angry ape,
> Plays such fantastic tricks before high heaven
> As make the angels weep. (25)

Huxley's view of man's essence is ascertained by the narrator who thinks that Love, Joy and Peace...are the fruits of the spirit that is man's essence and the essence of the world. But the fruits of the ape mind, the fruits of the monkey's presumption and revolt, are hate and unceasing restlessness and a chronic misery tempered only by frenzies are horrible. In *Ape and Essence* Huxley satirises more vehemently human civilizaiton, outcome of technological progress, which degrades to animal level.

Dystopian picture which Huxley presents, sounds to be a warning to people in technocratic era that if technological progress continues in the same way, irrespective of religious ethical, aesthetic, cultural, and political considerations, its resultant is the grim, horrible sub-human, post-catastrophe world. Mark Hilleges says:

> *Ape and Essence* is primarily a warning of how men, disregarding even their own self-interest, have set themselves in a direction which will lead ultimately to their own destruction. Either men, reproducing without limit and

> plundering their own planet, will eventually starve to death, or more likely they will turn their own technology, loose and ravage the world in a great holocaust.[32]

Huxley's fantasy about the nuclear catastrophe is materialised to some extent in the Second World War (1939-1945) with respect to the gruesome and horrible effects of nuclear explosions and radiation.

Huxley's dystopian vision of reality is explicitly mirrored in the nightmarish picture of the future world, and his approach to reality is that technological progress, to the exclusion of religious, ethical, aesthetic, cultural and political consideration, degrades and destabilises human society, and coupled with aggressive nationalism poses an uprooting threat to mankind to drag down the human existence into the abyss of the Dark Ages. He creates fantasy to serve his purpose of knowing meaning of reality. Fantasy reveals a new meaning of reality; fantasy is meaningful, and not absurd. The meaning of reality, which he understands, shocks readers who wholeheartedly insist on the glorious tomorrow based on technological progress.

VI

Stapledon makes fantasy acceptable to readers by providing rational ground to his fantastic hypothesis and he invensts the unfamiliar world with familiar places, human features, human reactions to make fantasy credible. Logic and inner consistency make the fiction acceptable to readers. Here fantasy is not opposed to reason. In 'other world' what he relates consistently is true and it accords with laws of that world and readers believe in it. In Huxley's case, once the basic assumption is accepted by readers, he creates the dystopian world of the future technocratic society with familiar, minute, precise and human details. In the strange and unfamiliar world, human emotions and feelings are real.

In the post-World War I, Stapledon has raised the British SF to epic grandeur, and attributed mythic dimension to it. Huxley has given dystopian turn to the British SF by creating the nightmare of the technological era. In the case of Stapledon, the connection between real and fancyful is very tenuous. He uses the basic hypothesis supported by existing knowledge in science as a take off point to create fantasy. Fantasy created on the assumption that it is "scientifically possible" does not necessarily have bearing on reality. This may, at the most, be treated as Stapledon's own vision and there is no reason why other should not treat it as purely fictional, utopian world having no link with the existing world. This is not a kind of fantasy which points to reality. He is optimistic about the spread of human race. Reflecting on human existence, he views that human existence in not altogether meaningless, and worth lies in his persistent struggle for survival. He uses fantasy as a mode to create myth. His mythic vision is that cosmos is without divine centre, and its creator is neither good nor evil. His utopian vision is that application of knowledge in science creates better world, and improves living beings. Unlike Stapledon, Huxley uses fantasy mode not to escape from the present world but to confront with it more daringly. He too employs the basic hypothesis as a take off point but in his case fantasy embodies the present world. Fantasy stresses; magnifies, and exaggerates contemporary tendencies. It is a kind of fantasy which points to reality. Like Wells, Huxley seems to approach reality from outside. He uses fantasy as a mode to create dystopian world. His dystopian vision of reality is that technological progress which ignores religious, etchical, aesthetic, cultural and political consideration, degrades and destabilises human society. To him, fantasy is a vehicle for satire.

REFERENCES

1. *Encyclopaedia Britanica* (London: Encyclopaedia Britanica Ltd.), Vol. 8, p. 916.
2. *Ibid.*, Vol. 13, p. 607.
3. Olaf Stapledon, *Last and First Men, Last Men in London* (London: Cox and Wyman Ltd., 1932) pp. 182-83 (Subsequent quatations are from this edition of the book, and are indicated in parantheses by page number/numbers).
4. H.G. Wells, *A Short History of the World* (London: Penguin Books Ltd., 1944), p. 255.
5. J. Salwyn Sachapira, *The World in Crisis* (New York: McGraw Hill Book Company, Inc., 1950), pp. 369-70.

6. H.G. Wells, *op. cit.*, pp. 256-57.
7. Leslie A. Fielder, *Olaf Stapledon: A Man Divided* (New York: Oxford University, Inc., 1983), p. 32.
8. *Encyclopaedia Britanica* (London: Encyclopaedia Britanica Ltd.), Vol. 11, p. 598.
9. Mark Hillegas, *The Future of Nightmare* (1967: rpt. Carbondale: South Illinois University Press, 1974), p. 140.
10. Chad Walsh, *From Utopia to Nightmare* (1962; rpt. Westport, Conn: Greenwood Press, 1975), p. 28.
11. Mircea Eliade, *Myth and Reality,* trans. Willard R. Trask (New York: Harper and Row,1963), pp 5-6.
12. Olaf Stapledon, Preface to *Star Maker,* (1937; rpt Harmondsworth: Penguin Books Ltd., 1973), p. 7. (The other quotation from the preface are from the same edition of the book, and are indicated by page number/numbers in parentheses).
13. Leslie A. Fielder, *op. cit.*, pp. 31-32.
14. P.S. Krishnamoorthy, *A Scholar's Guide to Modern American Science Fiction* (Hyderabad: American Studies Research Centre, 1983), p. 26.
15. J.O. Bailey, *Pilgrims Through Space and Time* (New York: Argus Books, Inc., 1947), p. 147.
16. Olaf Stapledon, *Star Maker* (1937; rpt. Harmondsworth: Penguin Books Ltd., 1973), pp. 41-42. (Other quotations are from this edition of the book and are indicated by page number/numbers in parentheses).
17. Patrick A. McCarthy, 'Star Maker: Olaf Stapledon's Divine Comedy', *Science Fiction Studies,* Vol. 8, 1981, p. 277.
18. Eric Rubkin and Robert Scholes, *Science Fiction: History-Science-Vision* (New York: Oxford University Press, 1977), p. 212.
19. Aldous Huxley, *Brave New World* (London: Chato and Windus, 1934), p. 117 (All subsequent quotations are from this edition of the fiction, and are indicated by the page number/numbers in parentheses).
20. *Encyclopaedia Britanica* (London: Encyclopaedia Britanica Ltd.), Vol. 6, p. 222.
21. Kenneth B. Melvin, Stanley L. Brodsky, and Raymond D. Fowler, Jr. *Psy. Fi. one: An Anthology of Psychology in Science Fiction* (Random House, Inc. 1977), p. 3.
22. Quoted from Mark Hillegas *The Future of Nightmare* (1967; rpt. Carbondale: South Illinosis University Press, 1974), p. 114.
23. John Timmerman, *Other World : The Fantastic Genre* (Bowling Green University Popular Press, 1983), pp. 16-17.
24. Mark Hillegas, *op. cit.*, p. 120.
25. Patrick Parrinder, *Science Fiction: Its Criticism and Teaching* (London: Methuen & Co. Ltd. 1982), p. 78.

26. *Encyclopaedia Britanica* (London: Encyclopaedia Britanica Ltd.), Vol. 2, p. 894.
27. *Encyclopaedia Britanica* (London: Encyclopaedia Britanica Ltd.), Vol. 9, p. 926.
28. *Encyclopaedia Britanica* (London: Encyclopaedia Britanica Ltd.), Vol. 23, pp. 191-191a.
29. Aldous Huxley, *Ape and Essence* (London: Chato and Windus, Second Impression, 1949), p. 49 (All subsequent quotations are from this edition of the fiction, and indicated by the page number/numbers in parentheses).
30. P.S. Krishnamoorthy, *op. cit.*, p. 130.
31. Harold L. Berger, *Science Fiction and New Dark Age* (Bowling Green, Ohio: Bowling Green Univerysity Popular Press, 1976), p. 7.
32. Mark Hillegas, *op. cit.*, p. 122.

C.S. Lewis and George Orwell

4

I

Chapter 4 concerns with the important SF writers like C.S. Lewis and Geroge Orwell, who contributed significantly to shape the genre in the post-Huxley period. The period was shadowed by the rumbling clouds of World War II and its dire consequences on human society. At the same time, the octopus of the totalitarianism in the garb of Fascism and Nazism had sprawled its tentacles. Besides World War II culminated into the dropping of the nuclear bombs on Hiroshima and Nagasaki. On the one hand, totalitarianism embarked on to subjugate humanity, and on the other, scientific progress, especially the nuclear science, posed a serious threat to human society. British SF writers, Herbert Best, Chambers Kearney, C.S. Lewis and George Orwell responded to these prominent changes. In Herbert Best's *The Twenty-Fifth Hour* (1940), the two scientific methods of destruction, the use of nuclear bomb to destroy the brain-centers of the modern state and a spread of disease germs specially bred for virulence bring a great collapse. Civilization is broken down over the world and mankind is on the verge of extinction. Troops of the United States reach Berlin and avert disaster. Chalmers Kearney's *Erone* (1943) has an earnest core of social analysis and practical suggestion for bringing about utopia. The utopian plan is based on two theses: (i) the need to create a world of abundance for all through economic, individual and scientific means, (ii) application of Christian principles in human life is necessary for human happiness. No doubt, Best and Kearney have used fantasy mode and contributed to British SF. Best has used fantasy mode to create dystopian world of the nuclear disaster. Kearney has employed it to create the utopian world which respects the Christian values. But after Huxley in

1930s and 1940s, the writers who used fantasy in their distinctive and effective ways are C.S. Lewis and Geroge Orwell. Serious disagreement with Stapledon's materialistic philosophy and his optimism that mankind will spread out across the universe with great benefit to itself and to the universe mark the SF of C.S. Lewis, the well-known Oxford Scholar of Medieval and Renaissance Literature. After Huxley's *Brave New World, Apes and Essence,* dystopia is retained in British SF by George Orwell. He has widen the horizon of British SF by creating the nightmarish picture of the totalitarian State in *Nineteen Eighty-Four* (1949). As such here efforts are directed to explore relation between fantasy and reality in C.S. Lewis's *Out of the Silent Planet* (1939), *That Hideous Strength* (1945), and George Orwell's *Nineteen Eighty-Four* (1949).

II

In the essay 'On Science Fiction', Lewis has divided SF into different sub-species. The first sub-species deals with leap into future when planetary or even galactic travel has become common. A SF writer criticises tendencies in the present world by imagining them to their logical limit. He does not see any objection to such a 'machine' in *Brave New World.* The second sub-species is what he called 'the Fiction of Engineers', and it accouts for Jules Verne's *Twenty Thousand League Under the Sea.* It is written by people who are primarily interested in space travel, or in any other undiscovered techniques, as real possibilities. The third sub-species is distinguished from Engineers' stories, and it envisages impossible world. The next sub-species is what he calls 'the Eschatological.' It is about the future, but not in the same way as *Brave New World.* This kind serves as an imaginative vehicle for speculations about the ultimate destiny of human species, for example, Wells's *The Time Machine,* Olaf Stapledon's *Last and First Men.* He turns at last to that sub-species in which he himself is interested and states his view:

> It is best approached by reminding ourselves of a fact which every writer on the subject whom I have read completely ignores. For the best of the American magazines bear the

> significant title Fantasy and Science Fiction. In it (as also in many other publications of the same type) you will find not only stories about space-travel but stories about gods, ghosts, ghouls, demons, fairies, monsters, etc. This gives us our clue. The last sub-species of science fiction represents simply an imaginative impulse as old as the human race working under the special conditions of our own time.... In this kind of story the pseudo-scientific apparatus is to be taken simply as a "machine".... The most significant appearance of plausibility—the merest sop to our critical intellect will do.... In all these impossibilites is, as I have said, a postulate, something to be granted before the story gets going. Within that frame we inhabit the known world and are as realistic as anyone else.[1]

To Lewis, SF is an imaginative impulse as old as the human race working under the present context, and here he links SF with myth. He thinks of SF as the mythic expression to explore deeper significance in relation to the present time. In *Out of the Silent Planet* (1938), a scientific device is space-ship which is used in the travel to the Mars. He does not provide a precise explanation of scientific mechanism of space-ship as Wells does in *First Men on the Moon.* Weston answers his kidnapped prisoner's question about the working of the machine as follows:

> As to how we do it—I suppose you mean how the space-ship works–there's no good in your asking that unless you were one of the four or five real physicists now living you couldn't understand: and if there were any chance of your understanding you certainly wouldn't be told. It makes you happy to repeat words that don't mean anything—which in fact, what scientific people want when they ask for an explantation—you may say we work by exploiting the less observed properties of solar radiation.[2]

Readers are not convinced by this type of evasive explantation of the mechanism of a flying machine. Though an explantation is evasive he infuses SF with vivid, familiar, and human details to make it credible. He describes the space-ship with vivid and familiar details. The ship is roughly spherical and the core of it is a hollow globe. The cabins are arranged inside it and their walls support an outer globe. Ransom while searching for a missing boy enters the room which is walled and floored with metal, and is in a state of continuous faint vibration—a silent vibration with a strangely lifelike and unmechanical quality about it. It is as if the metal chamber in which he finds himself is "bombarded with a small tinkling missiles." Ransom by now throughoutly frightened—not with the prosaic fright that a man suffers in a war, but a heady, bounding kind of fear that is hardly distinguishable from his general excitement. When Devine tells Ransom that loathsome sexless monsters will descend and he (Ransom) will be victimised, he is horrified. He sees in imagination various babulous eyes, grinning jaws, horns, stings, mandibles. A complex set of feelings arising out of loathing of insects, loathing of snakes and loathing of things play their horrible symphonies over his nerves. When he steps on Malcandra he feels that he is wandering on the moon's outer side, and irrationally enough, this idea brings him a bleaker sense of desolation. He experiences not only fear but also a ghostly inappropriateness when he is surrounded by dozens of Hrossa who are more animal and less human. They know navigation and poetry. Sorns are shepherds. A sorn's face is too long, too solemn and too colourless, and it is more unpleasent. A pfifltriggi has forehead and ears. Ransom notices that "part of its forelimbs on which it was supported was really, in human terms, rather an elbow than a hand" (130). Language which is the cultural feature of human society, is present on Malcandra, and these three species, speak the Malcandrian language. He invests 'other word' with familiar places and human details. Though 'other world' remains strange and unfamiliar the emotions and feelings are real.

Lewis's purpose of writing *Out of the Silent Planet* is explicitly revealed in his letter:

> What immediately spurred me to write...was Olaf Stapledon's *Last and First Men* and an eassy in J.B.S. Haldane's *Possible Worlds,* both of which seemed to take the idea of such [Space] travel seriously and to have the desperately immoral outlook which I try to pillory in Weston.[3]

Stapledon and Haldane present a materialistic philosophy that there is no heaven or hell, and the only hope man has of improving his lot through the application of the human mind—that is through science. Both works see man so applying his mind and thereby controlling evolution and eventually colonizing other planets. *Last and First Men* traces the future history of man through eighteen species. At the end, man cannot escape destruction. Stapledon leaves the Last men rejoining in their hideous pride and the task of seminating among the stars the "seeds of a new humanity." Last men conclude that "It was good to have been man." Stapledon's optimism that human race will spread across the universe and utopian outlook that science improves human race, are present in Haldane's essay 'Men's Destiny.' In this essay, Haldane states that our only hope of improvement is in science, and he fears that there will be opposition most likely from organised religion:

> If science is to improve man as it has improved his environment, the experimental method must be applied to him. It is quite lively that the attempt to do so well rouse such fierce opposition that science will again be persecuted as it has been in the past. Such a presentation may quite will be successful, especially if it is supported by religion. A world-wide religious revival, whether Christian or not, would probably succeed in suppressing experimental inquiry into the human mind, which offers the only serious hope of improving it.[4]

This strangling of scientific research before mankind has learned to control its own evolution, was for Haldane, a very strong possibility.

Lewis disagrees with Stapledon-Haldane idea about the future of human race. He does not stress this contemporary idea but employs it as a take off point to create an imaginary tale of space travel to Malcandra. He projects the immoral outlook of Stapledon-Haldane in the character of Weston. Weston, a physicist, a Stapledonian character views that it is the human right to invade other planet for the survival of human race, and hope for improvement of human race is in science and for that purpose any religious consideration is not important. Weston deploys his point of view:

> As far as we know, we are doing what was never been done in the history of man, perhaps never in the history of universe.

> We have learned how to jump off the speak of matter on which our species began; infinity, and therefore perhaps eternity, is being put into the hands of the human race. (29)

Ransom considers Weston's philosophy of life "raving lunacy." He disagrees with Weston's idea about vivisection. Devine curses Westorn for bringing him on Malcandra. Oyarssa comes to know the evil nature of Weston and Devine's obsession for the material pleasure. When Weston and Devine are captured for killing the three Hrossa, Weston extolls the superiority of the Thulcandrian civilization to the Malcandrian civilization and deciphers his intention to venture on Malcandra to Oyarssa:

> To you, I may seem a vulgar robber, but I bear on my shoulders the destiny of the human race. Your tribal life with its stone-age weapons and beehive huts, its primitive coracles and elementary social structure, has nothing to compare with our civilization—with our science, medicine and law, our armies, our architecture, our commerce, and our transport system which is rapidly annihilating space and time. Our right to supersede you is the right of the higher over the lower life. (157)

Weston's plea is that in the most crucial period in the human history it is worthy to shape the destiny of human race. To him, the human right is "the right of the higher over the lower life." He reiterates that "Life is greater than any system of morality; her claims are absolute (158)." He is convinced by the logic of improvement in the human history, and stresses the need of the continuation of the human struggle for survival, even though it supersedes the other living species. He is prepared without flinching "to plant the flag of man on the soil of Malcandra : to march on, step by step, superseding where necessary, the lower forms of life that we find, claiming planet after planet, system after system, till our posterity...dwell in the universe wherever the universe is habitable (159)." He is the representative of civilized man to place human life for ever beyond the reach of death by the names of interplanetary leap. Weston takes the idea of space travel seriously, and seems to have the immoral outlook. Donald E. Glover has commented in the essay 'Out of The Silent Planet' (1939) in *The Art of Enchantment* "The book is a romantic fantasy, a piece of science fiction.... It is focused on a space journey to a new world for the purpose of material and scientific exploitation."[5] Devine wants gold and Weston's scientific experimentation will lead to human colonization and consequently destruction of inhabitants.

In the case of Lewis, though fantasy thinly concerns with contemporary attitude about the future of human race in the immoral outlook of the Stapledonian protagonist, Weston, his main preoccupation is the creation of the world on the Malcandra which depicts Christian values. What is of seminal importance to him is his Christian vision. He provides an imaginary explanation for peace and order on the Malcandra and silence on the earth. He attributes mythical dimension to fantasy. On Malcandra, each order is ruled by the next higher order : beasts by hnau, hnau by eldila, and eldila by Maledil, the lord of all. On the other hand there is no Oyarssa to rule over human beings and each man on the earth intends to be a little Oyarssa. Oyarsa of Malcandra narrates about the silent planet, Thulcandra to Ransom:

> Once we know the Oyarsa of your world—he was brighter and greater than I—and then we did not know it, Thulcandra. It is the largest of all stories and the bitterest. He became bent that was before any life come on your world. Those were the Bent years of which we still speak in the heavens, when he was not yet bound to Thulcandra but free like us. It was in his mind to spoil other worlds besides his own. He smote your man with his left hand and with right he brought the cold death on my *harandra* before its time; if by my arm Maledil had not opened the *handramits* and let out the hot springs, my world would have been unpeopled. We did not leave him so at large for long. There was great war and we drove him back out of the heavens and bound him in the air of his own world as Maledil taught us. There doubtless he lies to this hour, and we know no more of that planet; it is silent (140).

Oyarssa of Malcandra gives the mythological explanation for the silence of Thulcandra. On Malcandra, the laws of pity and love prevail. Oyarssa of Malcandra does not permit human species to inhabit his planet. Weston and Devine are sent back to Thulcandra without killing them. Lewis does not prefer the idea of space travel to inhabit other planets to supersede other lives. By creating the 'Other World' on Malcandra, Lewis opposes Stapledon-Haldane ideas. Lewis's understanding of reality is that every being in the universe has right to live, and aliens in the universe are not hostile to the human world. Ramson becomes aware of superior celestial power which brings out peace and order on Malcandra. To him, the divine law operates in the universe. Unlike Stapledon Lewis believes that the universe is not without divine power. Donald E. Glover has observed that on another level:

> ...it is the story of long Christian's growing understanding of the truth of Deep Heaven, of other worlds, of planetary influences under the guidance of superior celestial powers and his growth into fuller manhood, an expansion of his knowledge and his soul. It is an attack on "Scientism" and a statement of the power of love, hope and chastity.[6]

To him, the book means the triumph of compassion, loyalty, obedience, and faith over the forces of greed, intolerance, egotism, and misguided idealism. Its message is entirely congruent with Lewis's romantic idealism and christianity.[7] Harold Shaw has rightly pointed out in the essay 'Out of the Silent Planet: The Discared Image', in *The Achievement of C.S. Lewis:*

> Perhaps one way of saying what Lewis's achievement is *In Out of the Silent Planet* would be to say that he has pressed the genre 'space fiction' into the service of ancient mythic and poetic themes—so much so that the designation space fiction no longer really applies very well, since at least part of which has occurred in the drama has been waking up, from its merely scientific tarper, of our notion what space is. The shift from space to Deep Heaven, and that to escape from the silence of our own world into the clarity and luminescence of another may be to find ourselves suddenly, face to face which our own history, only in a clearer light and with starker colours.[8]

The non-human super-power which advocates love, pity, obedience, goodwill, triumphs over egotism, arrogance, evil, greed.

In *Out of the Silent Planet,* fantasy ceases to be fantasy and SF acquires the dimension of myth. Lewis is thinly concerned with the contemporary problem and he uses it only as a take off point to create an imaginary world to unfold his religious vision.

III

In *That Hideous Strength,* Lewis's hostility to Stapledon-Haldane ideas becomes even more avert; there he shows what he believes will happen if these ideas are put into effect. He believes in objective values, that certain things are really true and other things really false about the universe. To abrogate these objective values is to violate a system of cross-cultural, universal ethics which Lewis collectively terms the 'Tao.' He asserts that the violation of objective values and the manipulation of nature are steps towards totalitarian rule; the soical, ethical and political conditioners who will assume power through the propaganding of their subjectivised violations of the 'Tao', are merely an extension of the 'Inner Rings' which Lewis consistently abhors. And political conditioners also avail themselves of science to perpetrate their ends; conquering Nature must, Lewis argues, end up conquering humanity ifself.[9] In *The Abolition of Man,* Lewis argues that the technological advancement exerts a certain toll upon the spirit of mankind. There neither is nor can be any simple increase of power on Man's side. He states "Each new power won by man is a power over man as well. Each advance leaves him weaker as well as stronger. In every victory, besides being general who triumphs, he is also the prisoner who follows the triumphal car."[10] In his letter on December 7, 1943 to Arthur C. Clarke, he states about his dissatisfaction with technology without ethical considerations:

> Look at Stapledon (Star Gazar ends in sheer devil worship), Haldane's *Possible Worlds* and Wasington's *Science and Ethics*. I agree technology is per as neutral: but a race devoted to the increase of its own power by technology with complete indifference to ethics does seem to me a cancer in the universe.[11]

Lewis disagrees with Stapledon-Haldane idea of technological progress without ethical consideration. He treats this contemporary idea as a take off point to create a hideous world of N.I.C.E. (The National Institute of Coordinated Experiments), and its destruction.

N.I.C.E. marks the beginning of a new era—the really scientific era. Feverstone tells Mark that the preservation of the human race is "a pretty rock-bottom obligation," and the interplanetary problem must be left on one side. The second problem is their rivals on the earth, animals like tigers, bears, elephants etc. The Third problem is man himself. He states, "Man has got to take charge of man. That means, remember, that some men have got to take charge of the rest."[12] Feverstone's policy is anti-human and he favours the dominance of same persons over the others, and disregards the individual human rights. He states his purpose, "Quite simple and obvious things, at first—sterilisation of the unfit, liquidation of backward races, selective breeding. The real education, inculding pre-natal education" (26). N.I.C.E. encourages scientific progress to make a new type of man by psychological conditioning of mind, biochemical conditioning of body, direct manipulation of the brain. Here the motif of the artificial creation of human being runs parallel to the making of the different classes of human beings by Bokanovasky Process in Huxley's *Brave New World*, and the creation of the Fifth Men by the scientific means in Stapledon's *Last and First Men*. To the public N.I.C.E. may seem no more than an attempt to have science applied to social problems and backed by the whole force of the state. Ultimately, it hopes to take over the human race, recondition it, control evolution, and finally make "man a really efficient animal." In other words, it brings about the situation of humanity being sung uner the conditioners which Lewis foresees in *The Abolition of Man*, Filostrato explains:

> This institue—Dio mio, it is for something better than housing and vaccinations and curing of cancer. It is for the conquest of death or for the conquest of organic life, if you prefer.... It is to bring out of that cocoon of organic life which sheltered the boyhood of mind, the New Man, the man who will not die, the artificial man, free from Nature. (104)

N.I.C.E. aims at the creation of a new type of man. In the context of the fiction it means cutting man away from the animal, turning him into a species of giant brains, something like Stapledon giant brains or Wells's Martians, and destroying as much of the organic life of the planet as possible. Straik says Mark "The resurrection of Jesus in the Bible was a symbol: to night you will see that is symbolised. This is real man at last" (105). In Bible, the resurrection of Christ is a beginning of a new era of light, love and goodwill, but N.I.C.E.'s experimentation marks a beginning of an era of darkness, hatred and evil, and that experimentation is without any ethical considerations. N.I.C.E.'s authority takes possession of Edgestow and it is instrumental to suspend the laws of England. Ramson states:

> ...that if this technique is really successful, the Belbury people have for all practical purposes discovered way of making themselves immortal. It is the beginning of what is really a new species...the chosen Heads who never die. They will call it the next step in evolution. And hence forward all the creatures that you and I call human are more candidates for admission to the new species or else it slaves...perhaps its food. (117)

To the scientists of N.I.C.E., a new human species is the next step in evolution, but to Ransom, it is victimisation of human beings to suppress individual human right and freedom.

Lewis makes use of the contemporary idea of Stapledon and Haldane marginally to create the hideous world of N.I.C.E. What he imaginatively conceives is of vital importance to him. To him, reality is what he constructs. He attributes mythical dimension to SF by interventation of supernatural agency for the destruction of N.I.C.E. Merlin, a magician, a super-human figure dug out of the land at Besbury is an instrumental to disrupt the plan of N.I.C.E., and speaks in a softer voice with Ramson, "Give me but seven days to go in and out and up and down and to and fro, to renew old acquaintance. These fields and I, this wood and I, have much to say one another" (175). Merlin liberates beasts like tiger, elephant, wolf, which are captured by N.I.C.E. Merlin kills Horace Jules, Wither, Straik and Filostrato. The metal ring is twisted, the rubber tubes are tangled and broken. N.I.C.E. which poses a threatening to human race is destroyed by super-human forces; a catastrophe is averted and evil is perished. The divine law operates in the garb of Merlin and because of that good triumphs and evil perishes. Unlike Stapledon, Lewis believes that divine power exists in the universe and it brings out victory of good and defeat of evil. He assigns religious significance to SF. His vision embodies religious aspect of reality than scientific one. In *That Hideous Strength,* Scholes and Rubkin views:

> Lewis created a scientific foundation, run by power-hungry bureaucrats, which threatened to usurp all power in England by its own clever manipulation of the media and its brutal modification of individual human beings.... But because these manipulators have no real values themselves, beyond a lust for power and personal satisfaction, their minds and souls are vacant. Into that vacuum the devil moves. The behaviorists in Lewis's novel are laterally possessed by devilish agents and behave accordingly. Their enemies are servants of God and accordingly inspired. The final combat is ultimate good against ultimate evil...and good wins easily.[13]

He has to assert that in the conflict between good and evil, the former wins. To Donald. E. Glover, on the highest spiritual level, the forces in opposition are those of Satan, the Bent Eldil of Thulcandra, operating through the medium of first, Wither, and the Head versus the powers, representing God and Maledil, who assist the human forces devoted to good in their battle to overthrow Satan. The battle in the conclusion is an unequal one, and the terrifying apocalypse which destroys Belbury and Edgestow places that hideous strength in the hands of the power which can legitimately and truly weild it.[14] Timmerman views that one attempts to rewrite the story by establishing one's own autonomy through man-made laws and structures which deliberately ignore the divine law, and "such a situation is depicted by C.S. Lewis in *That Hideous Strength* in which we find the dialectic between Logere, the community governed by divine law and Britain, the worldly community which abrogates divine law and supplants it with human autonomy."[15] Harold Shaw envisages the mythical meaning of *That Hideous Strength,* and asserts that the hideous strength which operates in the artificial manipulation of the head, irrespective of body, is the "Tower of Babel." He explores the link between N.I.C.E. and the Tower of Babel:

> Here, perhaps, is our first clue to the drama. Babel Chaos, Disintegration. And what was the particular nature of the disintegration at Babel? Was it not the breaking a part of language...say a breakdown between words and meaning, or the loss of the ability to attach intelligible meaning to things, a curse visited upon the race answering to its some of hubris. We will react a tower reaching to heaven. No. you will not (say the gods), for here is what will happen when you try to do this. Confusion. The connection of all this with the action in *That Hideous Strength* is that what starts out as an attempt on the part of the "Progressive Element" in Braction College to build a tower to heaven, ends up in a scene indistinguishable from Babel.[16]

In *That Hideous Strength,* N.I.C.E. which creates the "New Man" is destroyed like the Tower of Babel, by the divine power.

Lewis's SF is tenuously concerned with the problem in the contemporary world. Fantasy does not stress the contemporary issue seriously. Fantasy ceases to be fantasy and SF becomes mythical expression. He reconstructs elements of reality in order to put forth his vision. To him, reality is what he constructs.

IV

George Orwell's *Nineteen Eighty-Four* (1949) is a nightmare of totalitarian world. He shows how scientific machines as two-way telescreen, micorophones make a totalitarian state more powerful. Oceania, a totalitarian state is ruled by Big Brother; telescreens are installed in houses to watch the secret activities of masses, and for propaganda of the totalitarian ideology. Microphones are placed in houses and outside to hear even the low-pitched conversation. Once this basic assumption is accepted by reader, Orwell develops to create the unfamiliar, vivid picture of a totalitarian rule in 1984 in a realistic way. A state is divided into Oceania, Eurasia, and Eastisia, Oceania comprises the Americans, the Atlantic islands including the British Isles,

Australasia and the Southern portion of Africa. Eurasia comprises the whole of the northern part of the European and Asiastic land-mass. Estasia comprises China and the countries to the south of it, the Japanese islands and a large fluctuating portion of Manchuria, Mongolia and Tibet. Big Brother is never seen but his posters with the caption "BIG BROTHER WATCHING YOU" on the walls in the public places, and a voice from the telescreen, are familiar to the masses of Oceania. He is black-haired, black-moustachio'd, full of power and mysterious calm. Besides these familiar details, Orwell records human reactions of Winston. After his arrest, when he sees O'Brien entering the cell to torture him, he is shocked, whom he earlier deemed as his friend. When O'Brien tells him "you do not exist," the sense of helplessness assails him. In the final scene, when torture rises to cresendo, the cage of striving rats is brought nearer to him, he is extremely terrified and frightened. He fights furiously against his panic but in vain. There is a violent convulsion of nausea inside him and he becomes a screaming animal. There is one and only one way to save himself and that is to interpose another human being between himself and the rats. He shouts frantically over and over.

> "Do it to Juli! Do it to Juli! Not me! Julia! I don't care what you do to her. Tear her face off, strip her to the pones. Not me! Julia! Not me!" He was falling backwards into enormous depths, away from the rats. He was still straped in the chair, but he had fallen through the floor, through the walls, of the building, through the earth, through the oceans, through the atmosphere, into outer space, into the gulfs between the stars...always away, away from the rats.[17]

His hope for bright and open tomorrow is crushed cruelly and ruthlessly under the iron heel of Big Brother.

After World War I, the totalitarian tendencies had received momentum in the 1920s and the 1930s in the centralised governments of Joseph Stalin in Russia, and of Adolf Hitler in Germany. In 1928-29, Stalin defeated and expelled from the party, Trotsky, Zinoviev, and Kamener and their followers, Stalin turned against Bukharin, Rykov and Tomsky. He then effected a most drastic change of policy and began to industrialise

U.S.S.R., and to collective agriculture with a speed and ruthlessness which horrified even the original advocates of these policies. At the height of the industrial drive, shortly he introduced the quasi-liberal construction in 1936, Stalin staged great purge trials in which most of the old Bolsheviks and same military leaders were charged with treason, terrorsim and brought to confess guilt. Stalin exterminated the means which might have been able to overthrow him and form an alternative government during a national crisis. The purges carried out on a mass scale, imported to the Stalin regime its peculiar terroristic character. After a long series of purges and expulsion, Stalin succeeded in transforming the international into a "monolithic" organisation, identifying the interests of world communism with Stalin's dogmas and policies. Soviet scientists, writers, musicians, linguists, philosophers and other were made to accept his judgement as final.[18] Besides Russia, the totalitarian power emerged in Germany in the garb of the Nazi government of Hitler. Hitler gathered about him a group. of freebooters, political murderers and middle class riffroff. He organised Ordnertruppe of rowdies, which latter evolved into the brown shirted Strurmabtesslung (S.A.), with the black-shirted uniformed Schutzstaffel (S.S.) on a further refinement in the technique of political gangsterism. Between 1930 and 1932, Hitler's N.S.D.A.P., became the largest party in Germany. The rate of how he and his aids destroyed the German republic by treachery and deceit, built a totalitarian tyrat upon the foundations of intolerence and terrorism, rearmed the reich and ultimately enslaved Europe, is the tale of what Konard Heiden, perhaps Hitler's most acute biographer, once called "The Epoch of Irresponsibility."[19] Unlike other authoritarian states in history, the totalitarian dictatorship lacked all moral foundations. Being a government without any responsibility to man or to God, the totalitarian dictatorship justified any act of the state, no matter how monstrous. One illustration concerns communist Russia, which in carrying out its policy of collective farming restored to a "managed famine" in deliberately leaving millions of recalcitrant peasants to die of starvation by preventing aid from reaching them. Another concerns Nazi Germany, which in a carrying our racial policies deliberately exterminated six millions Jews by burning and asphyxiating them wholesale.[20] Orwell does not keep aside these totalitarian tendencies prevalent in the 1920s and the 1930s as insignificant, negligible part of the twentieth century reality. He cites explicitly his motive to write in his essay 'Why I Write':

> My starting point is always a feeling of partnership a sense of injustice. When I sit down to write a book, I do not say to myself, "I am going to produce a work of art." I write because there is some lie that I want to expose some facts to which I want to draw attention.[21]

He is dissatisfied with totalitarian tendencies in the present world and extrapolates his dissatisfaction into the nightmare of totalitarian rule in 1984.

In this SF, oceanic society is ruled by Big Brother and it has the different features of totalitarian rule. In Oceania, freedom of thought, freedom of speech, freedom of press, freedom of action, freedom of learning, are lost. Winston and Julia constantly change their hiding places to converse and act freely. Sex is a taboo in Oceania. The aim of the party is not merely to prevent men and women from forming loyalties which it may not be able to control. The poet, Ampleforth is arrested to hinder his freedom of expression; Rutherford, Jones, Aronson are vaporized for their thought crimes; the linguist, Synge is vanished and heard no more. Scientists are not allowed to carry out research on different areas which they prefer. Their areas of study are determined by the government's policy. There is no solidarity among scientists and writers. On the one hand, writers' words are silenced and on the other, scientists are mute spectators with an ice cold indifference for scientific progress. Hate-week is celebrated to arise hate and distaste among the inhabitants for Goldstein who advocates freedom. War is deemed as a device to maintain peace in Oceanic society. War means no more than a continuous shortage of consumption goods, and the occasional crash of a rocket bomb which may cause a few scores of death. Chocolate ration has restricted supply. War has economic purpose and it is to increase labour power. The strategic part of the totalitarian state is to treat ignorance as strength. Cut off from contact with the outer world, and with the past, the citizen of Oceania is like "a man in intersteller space, who has no way of knowing which direction is up and which is down" (204). The past is mutable. The mutability of the past is the central tenet of Ingsoc. A continuous alteration of the past is made possible by the system of thought which really embraces all the rest, and which known in Newspek (a language in Oceania) as "double think" which means the power of holding two contradictory beliefs in one's mind simultaneously, and accepting both of them. The Party intellecutal knows in which direction his memories ought to be altered; he therefore knows that he is playing tricks with reality. "Double think" is at the very heart of Ingsoc, science the essential act of the Party is to use conscious deception while retaining the firmness of purpose with complete honesty.

O'Brien says Winston, a staunch advocator of human freedom, dignity and rebel against the totalitarian rule of Big Brother that the power they have to fight for night and day, is not power over things, but over men. He continues:

> Do you begin to see, then what kind of world we are creating? It is the exact opposite of the stupid hedonisitc Utopias that the old reformers imagined. A World of fear and treachery and torment, a world of trampling and being trampled upon, a world which will grow not less but more merciless as it refines itself. Progress in our world will be progress towards more pain. The old civilizations claimed that they were founded on love or justice. Ours is founded upon hatred. In our world there will be no emotions except fear, rage, triumph and self-abasement. Everything else we shall destroy every thing. Already we are breaking down the habits of thought which have survived before the Revolution. We have cut the links between child and parent, and between man and man, and between man and woman. No one dares to trust a wife of a child or a friend any longer. But in future there will be no wives and no friends. Children will be taken away from their mothers at birth, as one takes eggs from a hen. The sex instinct will be eradicated. Procreation will be an annual formality like the renewal of a ration card. We shall abolish the orgasm. Our neurologists are at work upon it now. There will be no loyalty, except loyalty towards the Party. There

> will be no love, except the love of Big Brother. There will be no laughter, except the laugh of triumph over a defeated enemy. There will be no art, no literature, no science. When we are omnipotent we shall have no need of science. There will be no curiosity, no enjoyment of the process of life. All competing pleasures will be destroyed. But always—do not forget this, Winston—always there will be the intoxication of power, constantly increasing and constantly growing subtler. Always, at every moment, there will be the thrill of victory, the sensation of trampling on an enemy who is helpless. If you want to picture of the future, imagine a boot stamping on a human face for ever (273-274).

What the Party says is right and "the others were outside—irrelevant." The party seeks power only for its own sake. Because of the Winston's rebellious ideas he is electrically shocked; his body is actually pained by the pointed needle regulated by an instrument with a dial. His distorted, ugly figure is shown to him in the mirrors. He is transferred to Room No. 101 and ultimatley compelled to confess his guilt and love Big Brother. Jeffrey Meyers views that *Nineteen Eighty-Four* envisages man's fears of isolation, and disintegration, cruelty and dehumanisation. Orwell's repetition of obsessive ideas is an apocalyptic lamenation for the fate of modern man.[22] As Patrick Parrinder comments "Orwell Portrays a totalitarian society made possible by new forms of organisation, technology, and language.... It is an intentional, Swiftian distortion of various aspects of temporary society, ranging from the Nazis to British wartime rationing and the B.B.C."[23]

Unlike Huxley in *Brave New World*, Orwell in *Nineteen Eighty-Four* is more concerned with politics than with technology. The former is predominantly a technocratic hell and the latter political hell. Yet they have some resemblances. Each society is ruled by a small group of intellectuals. Each society accepts that social stability and freedom cannot live together. Each society makes use of applied psychology by conditioning mind. In both fantasies, the rebellion figures, the savage and Winston are tortured. Both depict the dystopian vision. Besides totalitarian tendencies, Orwell also satirises scientific progress. In Oceanic society, scientific researches are carried out to make the war machinery more advanced by inventing larger rocket bombs, powerful explosives, deadlier gases, disease germs. Science explores remoter possibilities such as "focussing the sun's rays through lenses suspended thousand of Kilometer away in space, or producing artificial earthquakes and tidal waves by tapping the heat of the earth's centre" (199). Machines are applied for evil purposes. Mark Hillegas observes that Orwell hates the nightmare of totalitarian power, obviously a great danger to human freedom and dignity. And yet there is hidden in *Nineteen Eighty-Four* consideable hostility to the machine. Oceania has the Utopia which machine civilization could bring. The monstrous world of 1984 could not exist without the machine, and in that nightmare world the machine serves only evil purposes: "From telescreens to helicopters, to the electric rack in the celler of the Ministry of Love, it is used chiefly as an instrument of surveillance, propaganda control, and torture. Orwell is saying that the machine makes a fully human life impossible."[24] Orwell's contention is that the stamping boot of the totalitarian rule crushes human spirit and moulds human character which craves for freedom and identity. To him, science can be powerful weapon to exploit human beings. This fiction poses a serious warning against totalitarian tendencies and scientific progress which freeze human freedom and dignity. J.R. Hammand has pointed out, "To see the book is a warning against totalitarian tendencies and attitudes is to recognise that it is not simply an anti-communist treatise: the society described is an amalgam of the worst features of both communist and Nazi regimes."[25]

Ninteen Eighty-Four raises a question whether it is to be called SF. Taking into consideration thin scientific content and more concern with the present world, it may be apt to call it a marginal SF. Though it is not SF proper it makes use of the science fictional device like the basic hypothesis supported by the known scientific knowledge to blow reality out of proportion. In it reality is presented in a magnified form. And this enlargement is not without purpose. The writer strategically employs the techniques developed by SF writers in order to develop the reader's awareness of the contemporary political problem. It enables us to view it in a more meaningful way. One gets the strong feeling of reality and not of fantasy. One may doubt whether it can be called fantasy. Fantasy is thin and what matters more is reality. Here he concentrates more on political reality than scientific one.

V

Lewis provides an evasive explanation to the basic hypothesis. He invests SF with familiar places, human features, human emotions and feelings to make it credible. In Orwell's case fantasy is based on the hypothesis which has rational ground. Orwell too uses the forementioned elements to make fantasy acceptable to readers but does not infuse SF with the supernatural as Lewis does.

Lewis disagress with optimism and utopian idea of Stapledon and Haldane. In Lewis's case fantasy ceases to be fantasy and SF becomes a mythical expression which depicts religious values. What he imaginatively conceives is of vital importance. To him reality is not what we see outside but it is what a writer constructs. Like Stapledon, Lewis is concerned with inner reality but their approaches to reality are different. Stapledon's vision encompasses material aspect of reality and Lewis's religious aspect of reality. His vision also reveals that scientific progress which remains indifferent to ethical values and religious values causes disorder in human society. In the combat between good and evil, good triumphs. In Lewis's case fantasy is thinly concerned with problems which we confront in the present world. Fantasy allows a necessary freedom to create 'other world' which embodies his vision. He infuses fantasy with supernatural. His purpose is not to satirise but to attribute Christian values to SF. Reality to which Lewis is related is Christian metaphysics. He unflinchingly is didactic in SF. In Orwell's case, if *Nineteen Eighty Four* is to be called fantasy, it is so in a loose sense of world because in it fantasy is thin, and what concerns more is reality and it makes constantly aware of the present world. Unlike Lewis, Orwell stresses; magnifies, and exaggerates contemporary tendencies into fantasy. Instead of turning away from problems in the present world, he confronts with them. In his case, fantasy and reality are closely connected. It is a kind of fantasy which closely links with reality. He uses fantasy as a mode to create dystopian world. Fantasy is a powerful weapon to satirise reality which we see outside. His dystopian vision is that totalitarian tendencies and scientific progress which disrespect human freedom and dignity destabilise human society.

REFERENCES

1. C.S. Lewis 'On Science Fiction' ed. Mark Rose, *Science Fiction: Collected Essays Twentieth Century View* (New Jersy: Prentice-hall Cliffs, 1976), pp. 110-13.
2. C.S. Lewis, *Out of the Silent Planet* (London: Pan Books Ltd., 15th printing, 1973), p. 27 (All subsequent Quotations are taken from this edition of the fiction, and are indicated by page number/numbers in parentheses).
3. Quoted by Roger Lancely Green in *C.S. Lewis* (New York, 1963), p. 26.
4. J.B.S. Haldne, 'Man's Destiny', *Possible Worlds* (New York, 1928), pp. 302-03.
5. Quoted from 'Out of the Silent Planet', Donald E. Glover, *The Art of Enchantment* (Ohio: Ohio University Press, 1981), p. 79.
6. *Ibid.*, p. 79.
7. *Ibid.*, p. 80.
8. Harold Shaw, 'Out of the Silent Planet: The Discarded Image', *The Achievement of C.S. Lewis* (Illinois: Wheaton, 1980), pp. 86-87.
9. C.S. Lewis, *The Abolition of Man* (New York: Macmillan, 1947), pp. 44-45.
10. *Ibid.*, p. 71.
11. Quoted from 'Out of the Silent Planet,' Donald E. Glover, *The Art of Enchanment* (Ohio: Ohio University Press, 1981), p. 76.
12. C.S. Lewis, *That Hideous Strength* (London: Pan Books Ltd., 12th Printing, 1973), p. 20.
13. Robert Scholes and Eric Rubkin, *op. cit.*, p. 47.
14. Donald E. Glover, *op. cit.*, pp. 112-13.
15. John H. Timmerman, *Other Worlds: The Fantasy Genre* (Bowling Green Ohio: Bowling Green University Popualr Press, 1983), p. 25.
16. Harold Show, 'That Hideous Strength: The Miserific Vision', *The Achievement of C.S. Lewis* (Illinois: Wheaten, 1980), p. 123.
17. George Orwell, *Ninteen Eighty-Four* (London: Heinemann Educational Books Ltd., 1965), p. 293. (All subsequent quotations are taken from

this edition of the book, and are indicated in parentheses by page number/numbers).

18. *Encyclopaedia Britanica* (London: Encyclopaedia Britanica Ltd.), Vol. 21, pp. 302-303.
19. *Ibid.*, Vol. II, p. 598A.
20. J. Salwyn Schapiro, *op. cit.*, pp. 246-47.
21. George Orwell, *Collected Essays* (London: Secker S. Warbug, 1961), p. 424.
22. Jeffrey Meyers, *A Reader's Guide to George Orwell* (London: Thomas and Hudson, 1975), p. 154.
23. Patrick Parrinder, *Science Fiction: Its Criticism and Teaching* (London: Methuen & Co. Ltd., 19), p. 75.
24. Mark Hilleges, *The Future of Nightmare* (1967: rpt. Carbondale: South Illinois Universely Press, 1974), pp. 128-29
25. J.R. Hammond, *A George Orwell Companion* (London: The Macmillan Press Ltd., 1982), p. 173.

Arthur C. Clarke and J.G. Ballard

5

I

Arthur C. Clarke and J.G. Ballard contributed significantly to shape the genre of SF after Orwell. Other SF writers are John Wyndham, Nevil Shute, Fred Hoyle, Brain Aldiss, and John Brunner. In John Wyndham's *The Day of the Triffids* (1951), mobile sentient plants threat to conquer the world, driving humanity into a tight corner. His *Chrysaldis* (1955) describes the rise of telepathically endowed race of human beings after a nuclear war. Nevil Shute's *On the Beach* (1957) portrays the end of the world through nuclear warfare. Fred Hoyle's *The Black Cloud* (1957) features a sentient alien in a from of a cloud that visits the solar system, which causes a great distrubance to human beings. When Michael Moorcock took over editorship of British SF Magazine, *New World* in 1964 from Ted Cornell, he directed the SF writers to create the 'New Wave' in SF and gave a clarion call to the SF writers who "reflect the pragmatic mood of today, who employ symbols gathered from the world of today, who use sophisticated writing techniques that of today, who employ characters fitted for the society of today."[1] British SF writers who responded to Moorcock's call are Brian Aldiss, John Brunner, and J.G. Ballard. Brian Aldiss's *Barefoot in the Head: A European Fantasia* (1969) describes a marathon journey across a dizzying psychodelic Europe ravaged by mind-shattering bombs. Brunner's *Stand On Zanzibar* (1968) is a terryfing over population projection of a near future extrapolated from the present trends. The writers who contributed significantly to enlarge the horizon of SF are Arthur C. Clarke and J.G. Ballard. In *Childhood's End* (1953), and 2001 : *Space Odyssey* (1968), Clarke harps on the theme of encounter of human beings with alien intelligences, but in different ways. His main concern is with the place and role of humankind in universe. The 'New Wave' in British SF finds its apotheosis in J.G. Ballard's writings. His *The Wind From Nowhere* (1962), *The Drowned World* (1962), *The Drought* (1964), *The Crystal World* (1966) are doomed worlds and they deal with the environmental disasters. They form a unique tetralogy and their connection is too obvious because in all four mankind perishes from the onslaught of element forces by air, water, fire and earth respectively. They are all doomed worlds. As such an attempt has been made to explore relationship between fantasy and reality in Arthur C. Clarke's *Childhood's End* (1953), 2001: *Space Odyssey* (1968), and J.G. Ballard's *The Drowned World* (1962), *The Drought* (1964), *The Crystal world* (1966).

II

Childhood's End envisages an encounter of aliens with human race. The fantastic hypothesis in the fiction is that universe is inhabited by aliens. In the *Exploration of Space*, Clarke writes "In the long run, the prospect of meeting other forms of intelligence is perhaps the most exciting of all the possibilities revealed by astronautics."[2] The basic assumption in this SF is that the universe is inhabited by aliens. Once this fantastic hypothesis is accepted by readers, Clarke creates the Utopian world guided by aliens, the Overlords. The planet, NGS 549672, from which the Overlords descend is described with scientific precision:

> This is a large planet–larger than Earth. Yet its gravity was low, and Jane wondered why it had so dense an atomsphere. He questioned Vindarten on this, and discovered, as he had half expected, that this was not the original planet of the Overlords. They had evolved on a much smaller world and then conquered this one, changing not only its atmosphere but even its gravity.[3]

'Other World' of the Overlords has resemblances to familiar places on the earth. Jan sees that the city in the world of the Overlords is certainly smaller than London or New York. After the arrival of the Overlords on the earth, there are significant changes like changing of trade routes into the intricate web-work covering the whole world, with no major nodal points.

London is still a centre of administration, of art, of learning. There are new bridges over the Thames, but in the old places. Nelson's solitary eye still stares down Whitehall's; the dome of St. Paul still stands above Ludgate Hill. Besides scientific precision, familiar details, human features and human reactions contribute to make fantasy credible. Aliens have resemblances with the human features like eyes, pupils, cheek, and thumb. The Overlords' faces have no trace of emotion. A narrator writes, "The great, wide, eyes, their pupils sharply contracted even in this indifferent light, stared fathomlessly back into the frankly curious human ones. The twin breathing orifices on either cheeks-emitted the faintest of whistles as Kerellen's hypothetical lungs laboured in the thin earth (134)." When Kerellen, the Overlord takes children away from the earth, majority of people experience terror. Clarke writes about the reactions of people:

> It was a tribute to Overlords psychology, and to their carefully years of preparation, that only a few people fainted. Yet there could have been fewer still, anywhere in the world, who did not feel the ancient terror brush for one awful instance against their minds before reason banished it forever (66).

Jan enters the Overlord system, he experiences disappointment, terror and his dwarfness. He is the first human being to look upon a world lit by another sun. In the city of the Overlords, buildings are lost among clouds. Streets are parctically non-existent and there seems to be no surface transport. The architecture of the Overlords are bleakly functional. Machines are beyond imagination. If a man from medieval times could have seen that red-lit city, and the beings moving through it, he would have certainly believed himself in hell. Even Jan, "For all his curiosity and scientific detachment, sometimes found himself on the verge of unreasoning terror. The absence of a single familiar reference points can be utterly unnerving even to coldest and clearest minds (193)." Jan saw that something else was rising out of the ruby clouds around the mountain's base. It was huge ring, perfectly horizontal and perfectly circular. Nowhere else on the world of the Overlords had seen such hues, and "his throat contracted with the longing and the loneliness they evoked" (199).

Being an astrophysicist Clarke was aware of the scientific progress in the field of rocket engineering from 1920s to 1940s In World War II, rockets loaded with nuclear bombs were used to blast the Japanese industrial cities, Nagasaki and Hiroshima in 1945.[4] He writes about the tragic ironies of our age:

> It is one of the tragic ironies of our age that the rocket, which could have been the symbol of humanity's aspirations for the stars, has become one of the weapons threatening to destroy civilization. This state of affairs has presented a difficult moral problem to those wishing to take an active part in the development of astrounatics, for almost all research on rockets is now carried out by military establishments and is covered by various security classifications.... Separating the military and the powerful uses of rockets is therefore an even more difficult task than creating atomic energy without atomic bombs.[5]

Clarke only takes cue from the contemporary tendency of the use of science for destructive purpose, and instead of confronting the problem in the present society he provides on imaginary exaplanation for the future of mankind after nuclear warfare. The Overlords arrive to stop men from turning their planet into a radioactive wasteland. Kerellen, the Overlord states:

> Your race had shown a notable incapacity for dealing with the problems of its own rather small planet. When we arrived, you were on the point of destroying yourselves with the powers that science had rashly given you. Without our intervention, the earth today would be a radioactive wilderness. (136)

Clarke has to assert that the applications of scientific progress for destructive purpose leads to end of human race. The Overlords, the superior aliens unite earth into one world. Under their rule, the earth becomes a technological utopia.

A new world, by the standards of all earlier ages, is utopia. Ignorance, disease, poverty, and fear have virtually ceased to exist. The memory of war is fading in the past as nightmare vanishes with dawn. When the Overlords have abolished war, hunger and disease, they have also abolished adventure and armed forces. The abolition of armed forces has at once almost doubled the world's effective wealth, and increased production has done the rest. As a result, it is diffcult to compare the standard of living of twenty-first-century man to that of any of his predecessors. The cities have been rebuilt or deserted and left as museum specimen when they have ceased to serve any useful purpose. The factories of robots are opened and production has become largely automatic. There are factories that run for weeks without being visited by a single human being. Men are needed for making decisions, for planning new enterprises. The robots do the rest. Crime has practically vanished. Another great change is the extreme mobility of the new society. There are plenty of technologists. Most people have two homes, in widely separated parts of the world. The polar regions have been made suitable for human habitation. A considerable fraction of the human race oscillated from Arctic to Antarctic at six-monthly intervals. Other has gone into the deserts, up the mountains, or even into the sea. There is no place on the planet where science and technology can not provide one with a comfortable home, if one wants it badly enough. Clarke says, "Utopia was here at last : its novelty had not been assailed by the supreme enemy of all Utopias...boredom" (75). The utopian world does not necessarily embody the elements of the contemporary world. Besides the Utopian world created by the Overlords, some people on the earth attempt to create 'New Athens' but their efforts are futile. Nothing in Athens is done without Committee, that ultimate hallmark of the democratic method. Robert Scholes and Eric Rabkin have commented on the nature of Utopia in *Childhood's End:*

> Clarke then in the New Athens, offers a Baconian corrective not merely to Plato's Athenian Republic but to the centralised and materialistic Golden Age. The democratized utopia has always been the alternative to the centeralised utopia, regardless of the possible attitudes towards technology. But in Clarke's novel, neither a centralised nor a democratized utopia emerges as a final answer for man. It is clear that the centralised utopia will fail through boredom; it is hinted that the democratized utopia will fail through human weakness (not everyone can

> even postulate pre-eminence as a goal, much less achieve it). Additionaly, both types of utopia only persist because of the protection and control of the science—stifling Overlords. Before either society has a change to weaken too seriously, however the mission of the Overlords is fulfilled.[6]

The Overlords' mission is to save human race from its destructive use of science, and they are triumphant in creating the utopian world by constructive use of science to restore harmony and peace on the earth. Clarke has to assert that scientific progress is not rival of human race but it is saviour of mankind.

After the restoration of harmony and peace on the earth, the next stage in the development of human race takes a different course. Human race is the fifth race whose apotheosis the Overlords have watched. Rashaverak, the Ovelord tells Jan, "We are the interpreters—the guardians or to use one of your other metaphors, we till the field untill the crop is ripe. The Overmind collects the harvest—and we move on to another task" (206). The Overmind uses the Overlords as a potter uses his wheel. Mutation takes place in children below the age of ten. Children who through mind energy alone remain in worldless communication with each other (by telepathic means), draw substenance directly into their bodies. As in epidemic, the metamorphosis infects the entire human race from land to land. It touches practically no one above the age of ten, and practically no one below that age escapes. Clarke writes in the third section of the fiction, 'The Last Generation':

> It was the end of civilisation, the end of all that men had striven for since the beginning of time. In the space of a few days, humanity had lost its future, for the heart of any race is destroyed, and its will to survive is utterly broken, when its children are taken from it. There was no panic, as there would have been a century before. The world was numbed, the great cities stilled and silent. Only the vital industries continued to function. It was as though the planet was in mourning, lamenting all that could never be. (179)

The Overlord brings out mutation in children on the earth. Taking away of children from the earth has broken the hope for human survival on the earth. The purpose for which the children are snatched away is not known. Clarke provides an imaginary explantation to the future of human race which faces a threat from nuclear disaster and SF acquires a dimension of myth. Myth of the future of human race reveals that aliens are intelligent and mysterious. Human beings are powerless before the mighty aliens. To Timmerman, the physical taking of the children, however, is only a symbolic act of a childhood that had been striped from the people long before. He views:

> While Huxley's dystopia is strident in its indicement against Scientism, Clarke's work is more of a mournful elegy for someone or something precious that has died. That something is man's humanity, the childlike which beats in the very fibre of humanity, the daring willingness to wonder.[7]

According to Dr. P.S. Krishnamoorthy, Clarke combines in this fiction, "an eschatalogical message, an ingenious explantation of the myth of the Devil, a speculative analysis of human destiny, and a projection of utopia society—all within the framework of a conventional alien encounter plot."[8] Frederick A. Kreuziger has observed in *Apocalypse and Science Fiction* that the myth-making process in our times is observed by the fact that we know the identity of the author—here refering sepcifically to SF and tend to interprete the process from the viewpoint of the author. To him, Clarke is one who "gives voice to the myth of total breakthrough and/or god-like transformation."[9] In *Childhood's End*, Clarke has created the myth of future of human race employing the motif of alien—encounter. Aliens in this fiction are powerful and intelligent than human beings. Clarke satirises human egoistic assumption that man is only intelligent and advanced being in the universe. Karellen views:

> In this galaxy of ours—there are eighty seven thousand million suns. Even that figure gives only a faint idea of immensity of space. In challenging it, you would be like an attempting to label and classify all the grains of sand in all the deserts of the world (136-137).

Human means are feeble to unravel mystery of the universe.

Wells in *The Time Machine,* deals with the future of human race. In it, he extrapolates and stresses the contemporary tendency of exploitation of workers to its logical consequence. But Clarke in *Childhood's End* does not strees contemporary tendency seriously. He envisages the contemporary situation only to provide a flimsy support to an imaginary tale of future of human race. SF becomes a mythic expresion which embodies the writer's vision of reality. To Wells, reality is that which we see in outside world while to Clarke it is what he perceives imaginatively.

III

Clarke was aware of the use of rockets in nuclear warfare in 1940s and its consequences on human society. He envisages it as a problem in the era of science and technology and states, "we must keep the problems of today in their true propositions: they are vital—indeed of supreme-importance, since they can destroy our civilization and slay the future its birth."[10] But he was optimistic about the use of rockets for exploration of space. He supports the opinion of Doctor Von Braum, an Honorary Fellow of the British Interplanetary Society, who views, "Let's hope that this was the last holocaust, and henceforth rockets will be used for their ultimate destiny...space flight!"[11] He thinks that the increasing pressure of population may bring about the conquest of the planets and indirect consequences of space travel will in fact help humankind to develop human world. He makes use of the contemporary problem to provide a ground to create an imaginary tale of encounter with aliens. He selects that aspect of contemporary society which deals with the advanced methods of warfare, population explosion and their serious effects on human society. Nuclear weapons are so powerful that they are efficient to destroy the inhabitants on the earth. Co-operation and peace are illusionary and there is storm underneath. Besides these aspects, octopus of increasing population spreads arms to destroy human race. Though birth control is cheap, reliable and endorsed by all the main religions, it has come too late; the population of the world is six billion—a third of it in the Chinese empire. As a result, food is short in every country; even the United States has meatless days, and widespread famine is predicted within fifteen years, despite heroic efforts to farm the sea and to develop synthetic foods.

Though Nuclear weapons, radiohypnosis, viruses, synthetic diseases in warfare are signs of scientific progress, there are also means for wiping out of the human race on the earth. Clarke has to assert that nuclear disaster and population explosion make the fate of human race more tragic and dark; human survival a difficult task. Consequently scientists on the earth are inclined to travel in space to search out an alternative for human survival, to unravel mystery of vast and unknown cosmos. He is too eager to wait for what is happening around. Once a thin link established with the present world, in Clarke's case, SF loses its contact with elements in it. The present world triggers off the writer's imagination to create an imaginary world of space travel and encounter with aliens.

The 'Other World' which he creates reveals attempts of human beings to conquer space and vastness of the cosmos. On the moon, Clavius Base is a closed system like a tiny working model of the earth itself recycling all the chemicals of life. The atmoshpere is purified in a vast 'hot house' ...a large, circular room buried just below the lunar surface. Under blazing lamps by night, and filtered sunlight by the day, acres of the green plants grow in warm, moist atmosphere. They are special mutations, designed for the purpose of replenishing the air with oxygen, and providing food as a by-product. All the necessities of life are produced from the local rocks, after they have been crushed, heated, and chemically processed. A narrator states:

> With the need for international co-operation more urgent than ever, there were still as many frontires as in any earlier age. In a million years the human race had lost few of its aggressive instincts; along symbolic lines visible only to politicians, the thirty-eight nuclear powers watched each other with belligerent anxiety. Between them they possessed sufficient megatonnage to remove the entire surface crust of the planet. Although there had been...miracuosly...no use of atomic weapons, the situation could hardly last for ever.
>
> And now, for their own inscrutable reasons, the Chinese were offering to the smaller have-not nations a complete nuclear capability of fifty war heads and delivery systems. The cost was under $200,000,000 and easy terms could be arranged.

> Perhaps they were only trying to share their sagging economy by turning obsolete weapon systems into hand cash, as some observers had suggested, or perhaps they had discovered methods of warfare so advanced that they no longer had need of such toys; there had been talk of radiohypnosis from satellite transmitters, compulsions viruses and blackmail by synthetic diseases for which they alone possessed antidote. These charming ideas were almost certainly propaganda or pure fantasy, but it was not safe to discount in any of them.[12]

Missiles are applied for the purpose of peace, and here Clarke satirises indirectly human tendency to use missiles for destructive purpose. Clavius Base is a miniature world itself. A narrator writes:

> With its complex of workshops, offices, store-rooms, computer center, generators, garage, kitchen, laboratories and food processing plant. Clavius Base was a miniature world itself. And, ironically, many of the skills that had been used to build underground empire had been developed during the half-century of the Cold War (39).

There are also mobile laboratories on the moon. A hundred million miles beyond Mars, in the cold loneliness where no man has yet travelled, radiation detectors note and analyse incoming cosmic rays from the galaxy. Neutron and X-ray telescopes keep watch on the strange stars that no human eye can ever see. Magnetors observe million-mile—a hour-blasts of tenuous plasma. Japetus is a disc about eight hundred miles in diameter and even in the lunar telescopes its disc is barely visible. Dr. Bowman says "but there seems a brilliant, curiously symmetrical spot on the face, and this may be connected with T.M.A.-I. I sometimes think that Japetus has been flashing at us like a cosmic heliograph for three hundred years, and we've been too stupid to understand its message"(101). Here he hints at limitation of human understanding. Saturn's many moons are frozen. Only one of them, Titan has an atmosphere and that is within envelop of poisonous methane. Saturn is surrounded by outer and inner rings of ice bergs. Will Bowman, a space traveller really appreciates its scale:

> But the glory of the rings continually dew Bowman's eye away from the planet; in their complexity of detail, and

> delicacy of shading's they were a universe in themselves. In addition to the great main gap between the inner and outer rings, there were at least fifty other sub-divisions or boundaries, where there were distinct charges in the brightness of the planet's gigantic halo. It was as if Saturn was surrounded by scores of concentric hoops, all touching each other, all so flat that they might have been cut from the thinnest possible paper. The system of rings looked like some delicate work of art, or a fragile toy to be admired but never touched. By no effort of the Will Bowman could really appreciate its true scale, and convince himself that the whole planet Earth, if set down here, would look like a ball-bearing rolling round the rim of a dinner-plate (109).

The Earth is smaller in scale as compared to that of Saturn. Alpha Centauri is the nearest of all alien suns, which is located beyond the solar system. He passed through star gate and he noticed that the sky above was stranger for there were no stars; there was the blackness of space. There was only a softly glowing milkiness, that gave the impression of infinite distance. Bowman remembered a description he had once heard of the dreaded Antarctic "whiteout." That sky could have no meterological effect of mist and snow; there was perfect vacuum there. He passed through a Grand Central Station of the Galaxy. He was light centuries away from the Earth. Most of the stars were concentrated in a glowing belt, broken here and there with dark bands of obscuring cosmic dust, which completely circled the sky. Bowman wondered "if this was indeed his own Galaxy, seen from a point much closer to its brilliant, crowded centre" (123). In a new system, a huge red sun, many times larger than the moon, shines in the sky. Here and there are rivers bright yellow as incandescent Amazons, meandering for thousands of miles. He saw pin-point of incandescene which must be a White-Dwarf-one of those strange, fertile little stars no longer than the Earth, yet containing a million times its mass. Like Stapledon, he, too, views that cosmos is vast and the earth is comparatively small. It is like a tiny speck in the panorama of cosmos.

In space travel, encounter takes place with aliens which are intelligent and mysterious. In space, the computer Hal

(Heuristically programmed Alagorithmic Computer) which contains artificial intelligences does not function properly. Hal's primary task is to monitor life-support systems; to check oxygen pressure, temperature. He is only aware of the conflict that slowly destroys his integrity the conflict between truth and concealment of truth. Deliberate error was unthinkable even the concealment of truth filled him with a sense of imperfection, of wrongness – of what, in a human being, would have been called guilt. For like his makers, Hal had been created innocent; but all too soon "a snake had entered his electronic Eden" (92). A narrator narrates:

> He had begun to make mistakes, although like a neurotic who could not observe his own symptoms, he would have denied it. The link with Earth, over which his performance was continually monitored, had become the voice of a conscience he could no longer fully obey. But that he would deliberately attempt to break that link was something that he would never admit, even to himself.
>
> Yet this was still a relatively minor problem; he might have handled it...as most men handle their own neuroses...if he had not been faced with a crisis that challenged his very existence. He had been threatened with disconnection; he would be deprived of all his inputs, and thrown into an unimaginable state of unconsciousness.
>
> To Hal, this was equivalent to Death. For he had never slept; and therefore he did not know that one could make again (92-93)...

He finds difficulty in linking with the earth and he has been threatened with disconnection. His very existence is challenged. Robert G. Pielke has observed in the essay 'Star Wars Vs. 2001: A Question of Identity':

> HAL is a brilliant and "self conscious" computer, which, as our progeny, necessarily incorporates our flaws as well as our creativity. HAL is programmed to accomplish a mission at all costs, but the programming conceals (by omission) the mission's true purpose: contact with alien life. This small variance from the "whole" truth was apprantely was not seen as a danger by mission control, even though the computer was given complete responsibility for operating ship. Alien contact was felt to be

far momentous for public awareness, and the crew might inadvertently reveal the truth if they knew. HAL is of course, "aware" of the contradictions, and the attempt to suppress it leads to errors and the resulting threat of disconnection - which would imperil the mission in house eyes.[13]

Because of distrubancy in the functioning of HAL, the space ship, Hull floats inert and motionless in the voild, like a tiny complex toy. Heywood Flyod from the earth communicates to Dr. Bowman, on the screen, "Two years ago, we discovered the first evidence for intelligent life outside the earth. A slab or monolith of hard, black material, ten feet high, was found buried in the crater Tycho. Here it is" (99). On the basis of the geological evidence it was three million years old. It was placed on the moon, when ancestors were primitive ape-men. The monolith is some kind of sun-powdered; or sun-triggered, signalling device. It has a powerful magnetic field. It is impossible to understand the motives of creatures three millions years in advance of human beings. He thinks, "The monolith may be some kind of alarm. And we have triggered it...." Floyd expresses:

> Whether the civilization which set it up still exists, we donot know. We must assume that creatures whose machines still function after three million years may build a society equally long-lasting. And we must also assume, untill we have evidence to the contrary, that they may be hostile. It has often been argued that any advanced culture must be benevolent but we cannot take any chances.
>
> Moreover, as the past history of our own world has shown so many times, primitive races have often failed to survive the encounter with higher civilizations. Anthropologists talk of 'Cultural Shock'; we may have to prepare the enitre human race for such a shock. But untill we know something about the creatures who visited the Moon and presumably the Earth as well...three million years ago, we cannot even begin to make any preparations. (100-101)

Here the presence of intelligent extra-terrestrials is overwhelming, and yet they are not visible. Clarke has to assert that aliens may be hostile or benevolent; they are mysterious. According to Robert G. Pielke, the aliens' purpose in *2001:*

Space Odyssey is beyond our understanding, because of "What they are and we are."[14] Rudoff Otto has alleged, "The truly 'mysterious' object is beyond our apprehension not only because our knowledge has certain limits, but because init we come upon something inherently 'wholly other', whose kind and character are incommensurable with our own..."[15] He has to assert that aliens' purpose is not exactly known. Their existence in space has mysterious appeal. Aliens are intelligent and powerful. Human knowledge has limit and it does not comprehend everything in vast cosmos.

In Clarke's case, fantasy ceases to be fantasy and it becomes an imaginary tale of space travel. The world which he imaginatively conceives has a less common ground with the present world. The 'Other World' provides a necessary freedom for Clarke to put forth his vision of cosmos. It does not confront the present world more daringly to view it in a new perspective. What is of seminal importance to him is not the present world but his vision which unfolds his understanding of reality. To Clarke, reality is not what we see in the outside world but it is within.

IV

Ballard contends that SF, owing to its specific genre features, has an exceptional abililty to raise the burning problems of our day. He views that the traditional themes existing before the 1960s...visitants from the other planets, space flights, and travel into the remote future...could not adequately render the tragic complexity of an individual's life in modern society. Exploring the inner world of man is far more important task for a science fiction writer than portraying outer space. One of the main purposes of SF, Ballard views, is to account for the changing psyche of a man living in the age of science and technology.[16] It is clear that Ballard aims at providing psychological dimension to SF.

The Drowned World is an environmental catastrotopic fiction and in it destructive agent is excessive water. The fantastic assumption in this SF is that change in solar activity increases temperature which melts the polar ice-caps and floods much of the earth's surface. It is based on rational ground. In the geological history of the earth, there was the Glacial epoch of the Ice age which was the sixth of the seven epochs that constitute the Cenozoic era of geological history. *Encyclopedia Britanica* Vol.10 contains its definition and the changes associated with it:

> It is defined as the epoch of alternating glacial and interglacial ages when, during the glacial ages, widespread continental ice sheets repeatedly affected large areas in the northern hemisphere and alpine glaciers were more numerous and extensive in both the northern and southern hemisphere. During the interglacial ages the climate was as warm or warmer than the present, soils were formed and the glaciated areas were reclothed with vegetation and repopulated with animal life. This epoch is believed to have lasted roughly 1,000,000 years. It is generally regarded as having been terminated by the melting away of the latest of the great sheets.[17]

Besides this geological reality, in the present time, the environmental reality is that Ozone layer in environment is becoming thin and so most of the sunrays reach on the earth, without hindrance and consequently the temperature on the earth is increasing. Once a fantastic hypothesis based on a rational ground is accepted by readers, he creates a new conceptual world which he infuses with familiar places, human emotions and feeling.

The continued heating of the atmosphere begins to melt the polar ice-caps. The entranced ice-seas of the Antarctic plateau breaks and dissolves, tens of thousands of glaciers around the Arctic Circle, from Greenland and Northern Europe, Russia and North America, pours themselves into the sea, millions of acres of permafrost liquified into gigantic rivers. While surveying the lagoons, Bodkin asks Kerrans about a place where they have arrived. When Kerrans shook his head he says "part of it used to be called London; not that it matters. Curiously enough, though I was born here. Yesterday I rowed over to the old University quarters a mass of little creeks, laboratory, water was already ankle-deep through the scuppers, sluicing among the sinks and benches."[18] Besides familiar places, human emotions and feelings recorded are real. Reptiles in lagoon create fear in the mind of Kerrans. He is aware of Stragman's malice and unpredictability, he feels confident that he will not try to kill him by so crude a method as blocking the air supply. He sees Stragman in an immense ballooning space-suit before him ten feet away, "white bubbles streaming from his frog-like head, hands raised in an attitude of menace, a blaze of light pouring from his helmet (107)," with a shock of alarm. When Kerrans moves on southwards, he experiences loneliness and nightmare. A narrator writes:

> The sea was no longer visible, and he was alone with these few lifeless objects, like the debirs of a vanished continuum, one dune giving way to another as he dragged the heavy fifty-gallon drums from crest to crest. Overhead the sky was dull and cloudless, a bland impassive blue, more the interior ceiling of some deep irrevocable psychosis than the storm-filled celestial sphere he had known during the previous days. At times, after he had dropped one burden, he would totter down into the hollow of the wrong dune, find himself stumbliing about the silent basins, their floors cracked into hexagonal plates, like a dreamer searching for an invisible door out of his nightmare (168).

Kerrans, Dr. Bodkin and Beatrice Dahl are lonely and disparing people. V. Gopman has commented on their mental state:

> And although their mental state is given a "science-fiction explanation," the real reason lies in that primary feeling of anguish and despair which, in Ballard's opinion is genetically present in man and which the awakening of a genetic memory brings out from the depths of his subconsciousness.[19]

Though a conceptual new world is unknown, human reactions provide an authenticity to it.

Ballard is aware of mid-century man shattered by the horrors of World War II, and the nightmare pertaining to the nuclear explosion in 1945.[20] Besides the nuclear catastrophe, he becomes conscious of a diverse effects of environmental imbalance. To him, the psyche of a man who goes through the tragic changes in the age of an essentially new technology an essentially new environment is a serious sign of the present reality.[21] He extrapolates this aspect of the contemporary society into fantasy by creating vivid, apocalyptic picture of the world drowned by the flood-water.

A series of violent and prolonged solar storms lasting several years, caused by a sudden instability in the sun diminished the earth's gravitational hold upon the outer layer of the ionosphere which results into rise in temperature. The change in solar activity melts the polar-caps and turns the world into one great swamp. Entire Europe turns into a system of lagoons. Flood-water has disastrous consequences on human beings. In the drowned world, water is an apple of discord and its life-giving power is lost. X-Anopheles causes malaria and skin cancer is frequent. During the next thirty years the poleward migration of population continues. A few fortified cities defy the rising water-levels and the encroaching jungles, build elaborate sea-walls around their perimeter, but one by one these are breached. Cities on higher grounds in mountains areas nearer the Equator are abandoned, despite their cooler temperature because of diminished atmospheric protection. The steady decline in the mammalian fertility, and the growing ascendancy of amphibian and reptile forms best adopted to an acquatic life in the lagoons and swamps, invert the ecological balances. The birth of a child has become a comparative rarity, and only marriage in ten yielded any offspring. As Kerrans sometimes reminded himself "the genealogical tree of mankind was systematically pruning itself, apparently moving backward in time, and a point might ultimately be reached where a second Adam and Eve found themselves in a new Eden" (23). Dome and theatre are submerged. The big dome is about twenty feet below water and in the centre of the dome the water is at least twenty degrees warmer than it has been in the control-room. When the barrage is blown, a narrator writes about the destructive role of water:

> Widening as he (Kerrans) watched, the water jetted down into the open states below, carrying with it huge sections of the slit bank. There was a concerted rush to the deck of the depot ship, a dozen arms pointing up at the water pouring out of the

> breach. It swilled into the square, only a few feet deep, blotting out the fires and splashing against the hull of the ship, still rocking slightly from the impact of the explosion.
>
> Then, abruptly, the lower section of the barrage fail forwards, a brace of a dozen twenty feet logs going down together. The ushaped saddle of slit behind collapsed in turn, exposing the full bore of the inlet creek, and what appeared to a gigantic cube water fifty feet high tipped into the street below like a flopping piece buildings, the sea poured in full flood. (163)

Stragman asks Kerrans where they would go. There is nothing left much then. He feels like the phlebas the Phoenician because he experiences drowning in water, and for him, water has lost its function of regeneration.

In The Drowned World, landscape has distinctive role to play and it has disastrous effect on human personality. External landscape is psychologically related to the characters in the SF. The scientist Bodkin argues that the return of the primeval climate heralds a decisive psychic transformation:

> I am convinced that as we move back through geophysical time so we re-enter the amniotic corridor and move back through spinal and archaeopsychic time, recollecting in our unconscious minds the landscape of each epoch, each with a distinct geological terrain.... [This is] a total re-orientation of the personality. (44)

Environmental change triggers off psychic change. Hardman is no more than a resurrected corpse, without food. When Hardman counts his last days, Kerrans feels that his (Hardman's) real personality is submerged deep within his mind, and external responses are nearly "pallid reflections of this, overlayed by his delirium and exposure symptoms" (173). He tells Bodkin that in response to rise in tremperature, humidity and radiation levels, the flora and fauna of the earth are beginning to assume once again the forms they displayed the last time such conditions were present...in the Triassic Period. However, selective the conscious mind may become most biological memories are unpleasant ones, echoes of danger and terror. Everywhere in nature one sees evidence of innate releasing mechanisms literally millions of years of old, which have been dormant through thousand of generations but retained their power undiminished. We all carry within us a submerged memory of the time when the giant spiders were lethal and when the reptiles were the planet's dominant life form. He highlights the relation between the present environmental catastrophe and past:

> There are the oldest memories on the earth, the time-codes carried in every chromosome and gene. Every step we have taken in our evolution is a mile stone inscribed with organic memories...from the enzymes controlling the carbon dioxide cycle to the organisation of the branchial plexus and the nerve pathways of the Pyramid cells in the mid-brain, each is a record of a thousand decisions taken in the face of sudden physico-chemical crisis. Just as psychoanalysis reconstructs the original traumatic situations in order to release the repressed material, so we are now being plunged back into the archaeopsychic past, uncovering the ancient taboos and drives that have been dormat for epochs. The brief span of individual life is misleading. Each one of us is as old as the entire biological kingdom and our bloodstreams are tributaries of the great sea of its total memory. The uterine odyssey of the growing foetus recapitulates the entire evolutionary past, and central nervous system is a coded time scale, each nexus of neurones of each spinal level making a symbolic station, a unit of neuronic time (44).

The drowned world instigates Kerrans and Bodkin to enter into the archaeopsychic past. It recalls memories which are dormant through thousand of generations.

In Kerran's case, the distinction between the latent and manifest contents of the dream are ceased to be valid. The terrestrial and psychic landscape are indistinguishable, as "they had been at Hiroshima and Auschwitz, Golgotha and Gomorrah" (74). Dr. P.S. Krishnamoorthy has pointed out "*The Drowned World* (1962) in which melting polar ice devastates the world and drives the people to scavenge for flotsam and in jetsam of the past and recalls racial memories in their dreams."[22] In Ballard's SF external landscape and the psychic state of characters are related. V. Gopman has viewed that in this fiction Ballard is preoccupied "with the state of his heroes, with establishing the correlation of their inner world, their mental state, and "inner landscape" with the "external landscape" of the drowned world.[23]

In the catastrohic world, human efforts are futile. The United Nations attempt to move the remaining human population to the polar regions, where it is hoped "life would continue much as before, with the same social and domestic relationships, by and large the same ambitions and satisfaction." But Kerrans and his campanions refuse to go; they know that the old order is dying, that in the primeval jungles, there is a place for traditional values. The efforts of Kerrans and Bodkin are futile to avert the environmental catastrophe. Stragman resembles other character as Lomax. There are representatives, in varying degrees, of the greed, the lust for power, and the fascination with techonology characteristic of the twentieth century of civilisation. All flourish in an urban environment, all challenge nature with their technology and their masterful personalities, and all, ultimately are failures. Besides the failures of human efforts, human relationships break in the drowned world. There are no meaningful relations between Kerrans and Beatric Dahl, or between Kerrans and Bodkin. Each of these characters is isolated, exploring his or her own inner universe. When Kerrans intends to go southward, he tells Betrice, "Darling, where are you going. I'm sorry, I cann't be with you (165)." In spite of the breaking of human relationship with Betrice, Kerran searches for new order:

> So he left the lagoon and entered the jungle again, within a few days was completely lost, following the lagoons southward through the increasing rain and heat, attacked by alligators and giant bats, a second Adam searching for the forgotton paradises of the reborn son. (171)

Ballard has said that "in a novel like *The Drowned World*... the hero is the only one who is persuing a meaningful course of action."[24] Clearly, Ballard is suggesting that his hero will be reborn (i.e. under a psychic transformation) in the jungle or desert; yet both Kerrans and Sanders follow courses of action that seem certain to cause their deaths. David Norman Samuelson in his doctoral thesis entitled *Studies in Contemporary American and British Fiction* has commented:

> *The Drowned World* has equally mysterious catastrophe, but it focuses on one man and his reactions. The biologist Robert Kerrans, gradually succumbs to the lure of the South, the sun, and prehistoric past which, in making dreams, dominate his meager existence in a world where only the polar regions are fit for human habitation.[25]

Ballard's picture of apocalyptic world is not completely bleak and nightmarish but has a glimmer of hope. Ballard's apocalyptic vision of reality is that in modern time of science and technology, water has no life-giving power, and it is a source of destruction and not of regeneration. External landscape triggers off psychic transformation in human beings. Human efforts are futile to avert catastrophe. Besides the futility of human efforts, human relationships break in the grip of the environmental disaster.

In this SF, fantasy extrapolates; stresses the environmental aspect of contemporary society to view it in a more meaningful way. Fantasy points at reality. Ballard's apocalyptic vision of reality warns readers to avert catestrophe. It works as a curative.

V

J.G. Ballard's *The Drought* (1964) is an environmental catastrophe which deals with the contemporary problems of water pollution. The basic assumption in this SF is that water pollution causes a global disaster of drought. This fantastic assumption is based on the scientific fact that the different industrial wastes are pumped into rivers or seas. Drought is set in a near future when nuclear and industrial wastes have covered the oceans, preventing evaporation and leading to world-wide aridity. In *The Drought,* fantasy stresses and magnifies the problem of water pollution due to industrial wastes in the present society to create the world of environmental catastrophe. Millions of tons of highly reactive industrial wastes—unwanted petroleum factions, contaminants, catalysts and solvents—are vented into the sea, where they mingle with the wastes of atomic power stations and sewage schemes. Out of that brew the sea has constructed a skin "no thicker than a few atoms, but sufficiently strong to devastate the lands it once irrigated (44)." The World-wide drought is the culmination of a series of extended droughts that have taken place with increasing frequency all over the globe. A narrator says:

> Covering the off-shore waters of the world's oceans, to a distance of about a thousand miles from the coast, was a thin but resilient mono-molecular film formed a complex of saturated long-chain polymers, generated within the sea from the vast quantities of industrial wastes discharged into the ocean basins during the previous fifty years. This tough, oxygen-permeable membrane plays on the air-water interface and prevented almost all evaporation of surface water into the air space above.[26]

A mono-molecular film on water surface stops evaporation of water and consequently causes drought. Water scarcity is prevalent everywhere and it culminates into the world-wide drought. A critical shortage of World food-stuffs has occurred when the seasonal rainfall expected in a number of important agricultural areas has failed to materialize. A survey by the U.N. Food and Agriculture Organization shows that everywhere river level and water level fall. The two and a half million square miles drained by the Amazon has shrunk to less than half this area. Aerial surveys discover that the much of the former rain forest is already dry and petrified. Dr. Ransom surveys the drought affected areas and observes the corpses of hundred of fishes, voles and water fowl among the weeds. He encounters with seventy-five years gray-haired old negro and tells him that they must go to the south of the coast, but the old negro says, "I shall be a great burden to you doctor. I would rather stay here than be left by the roadside later. May I ask you to be honest with yourself:" (117). The Words of the negro reveal that humanitarian consideration are becoming irrelevant in the catastrophic world. Later on the old negro is died because of scarcity of water. There are no signs of movement of the wharfs and riverside streets but the roads are deserted. Mount Royal and Hamilton are burnt and people leave those areas. Ransom thinks of the whole world as a kind of disaster area. This motif, of the world as a "disaster area" characterises Ballard's SF.

In the catastrophic world, brutal struggle for existence prevails due to an acute shortage of water. When Ransom reaches the sea coast, Grady claims for his priority for water. A narrator says:

> The scattered shooting resumed, the soldiers firing over the heads of the hundreds of people moving straight towards the sea. Taking Catherian by the arm, Ransom pulled her towards the opening in the inner fence. Behind them, more bodies lay among the dumes, tumbled awkwardly in the coarse grass.

Following an empty creek, they moved from the huts. As they crouched down rest before their final dash to the sea, man stood up in the blunt grass ten feet above them. With a raised pistol he began to fire across the dunes, shooting straight at the people driven back by the soldiers.

> Looking up at him, Ransom recognised the stocky soldiers and pugnacious face. 'Grady!' he called. 'Hold off, man!' As they stumbled from their hiding-place Grady turned and searched the darkness below him. He levelled his pistol at them. He seemed to recognise Ransom, but gestured at him with the weapon.
>
> 'Go back!' he shouted hoarsely. 'Keep off, we come first!' (142).

Because of Grady's arrogance, Ransom turned serious and shot him. Besides Grady, Lomax putting on a show of dignity warns Ransom not to steal water:

> He (Ransom) looked up to find Lomax grimacing over him, silver-topped cane in one hand. 'Ransom....!' he hissed. 'Get out.... !'. His suit was puffed up, the lapels flaring like the gills of an angry fish. 'You're stealing my water! Get out!' (242).

Lomax was stunned by the horror of this island infested by nightmares. To Lorenz J. Firsching, "In sea side communities, water is a medium of exchange...and thus the instrument of exploitation. On the banks of the dying river (which Ransom has temporarily abandoned) Lomax...controls the remaining water as a means of controlling those around his : so that water here becomes a medium or instrument for exercising political/ economical power."[27] Lomax is obsessed with power and technology within urban environment. He resembles with Stragman in *The Drowned World.*

In this SF too, external landscape has bearings on the psychic states of the characters. A landscape here is arid and deserted. Dr. Ransom observes:

> The heat of waterfront fires drove across the river like a burning sirocco. The entire horizon was ablaze, enormous fires raging on the outskirts of the city. Hamilton burned along the northern bank of the river, the flames sweeping down the streets. The boathouses by the grayes were on the fire, the hundreds of fishes illuminated in the dancing light.... Overhead, myriads of glowing cinders sailed past like fire files, and lay in the field to the south as if the soil itself was beginning to burn. (119).

As they near the harbour, burnt-out roofs rise above the warehouses by the dockyards. Ransom looks up at the wharfs and riverside streets, waiting for any signs of movement, but the roads are deserted, canyon floors fill with sand, and "the building reached in the dusty tiers, transforming Mount Royal into a pre-historic terrace city, a dead metropolis that turned its forbidding stare on them as they passed" (208-209). Arid and deserted landscape initiates Ransom to feel that "he was advancing across an inner landscape where the elements of the future stood around him like the objects in a still life, formless and without associations" (197). Commenting on the environmental catastrophe in *The Drought,* Gopman says:

> not only the physical constant of the human environment is destroyed, but also the constant which, in Ballard's view, connects the physical world with the mental. There is the destruction of Ransom's psyche, the burnt-out world about him, and in addition the feeling that time has stopped, broken off.[28]

In this SF, Ballard's correlates 'inner landscape' with 'external landscape', the tragedy of perishing world keeps pace with psychological catastrophe of the personages, and herein lies the book's centre of gravity. In Ballard's case devastated landscapes function, to some degree, as metaphorical reflections of man's inner landscape.

Human efforts are futile in the grip of the global drought. Despite world-wide attempts at cloud-seeding, the amount of rainfall continues to diminish. The seeding operations finally end when it is obvious that there is no rain and there are no clouds. At that point attention switches on to the ultimate source of rainfall—ocean surface, but efforts are feeble to save human race from water scarcity. Although the structure of the polymers is quickly identified, no means are operable to control their formation. The saturated linkages are completely non-reactive, and form an intact seal broken only when the water is violently disturbed.

Besides the futility of human efforts, human relationship is also failure in the catastrophic world. "The failure of Ransom's marriage", Ballard remarks, is primarily "that of its urban context, in fact a failure of landscape" (11). With his discovery of the river Ransom finds an environment in which he feels completely at home, a zone of identity in space and time. The river is a "great moderator" which "casts its bridges between all animate and inanimate objects alike" : but "with the death of river, so would vanish any contact between those stranded on the drained floor" (11). The draining of river does not create any physical barrier between the people living on its banks and floor but Ransom is convinced their relations will end. The death of river is connected with the death of personal relations, with isolation. Lomax sees a future in the city, describing it as a "phoenix"; he proceeds to make this analogy good by burning down the city as "the prelude to even greater futures" (44). The conflagration proves to be a psychic release for Ransom. It liberates him to undertake his long delayed trip to the sea side community, where he renews his relationships with Judith. But that new relationship once again fails, perhaps again because of "a failure of landscape."

In this SF, the catastrophic world is coupled with the birth of new order in the end. Quilter, the harbinger of the new order destroys Lomax's reservoir. Shortly after that act of destruction aimed at the old order, a rain starts to fall, which hints at the birth of new order. His approach to reality is that environment in the face of calamity is unsympathetic and hostile. Technology's challenge to environment leads to global disaster. In the grip of the dier environmental calamity human efforts are failures and human relations break. Darkness is lined by a ray of light. He poses a warning to readers who assume that technological progress saves human race.

Ballard has attributed the psychological dimension to SF. He has employed fantasy as a mode to create apocalyptic world which embodies the elements of present society. Fantasy stresses; magnifies reality to view it in a more meaningful way. Fantasy is not turning away from reality but it is a powerful weapon to apprehend reality. In his case, fantasy points to reality.

VI

As it has been pointed out earlier Ballard is dissatisfied with environmental imbalance and the shattered psyche of modern man. In Tobaco Mosaic, the plant tissues form crystal like structures due to viral infection. Ballard selects this element from the contemporary world and magnifies; exaggerates it to create the crystalised world.

The fantastic assumption in the fiction is that crystalisation of living tissues prevails due to environmental changes and it causes a global disaster. The plants in the forest of Mount Royal form crystal structures, fifty miles up the Matare River. But that is not the only affected area in the world. The other affected sites are in the Florida Everglades, and the Pripet Marshes of the Soviet Union. Crystalization of forest advances at the rate of some four hundred yards each day. The crystal trees in the forest are glass-like trellises of moss. Everywhere the forest is motionless in the warm air. The long arc of trees hanging over the water seem to drip and glitter with myriads of prisms, the trunks and branches sheathed by bars of yellow and carmine light that bleeds away across the surface of the water. The entire length of the opposite shore glitter with the blurred kaleidoscope, the overlapping bands of colour increasing the density of the vegetation. Dr. Sanders sees that scenario of the crystalisation of the plant tissues in the river water:

> Extending outwards for two or three yards from the bank were the long splinters of what appeared to be crystalizing

> water, angular facets emitting a blue and prismatic light washed by the wake from their craft. The splinters were growing in the water like crystals in a chemical solution, accreting more and more material to themselves, so that along the bank there was a congested mass of rhomboidal spears like the barbs of a reef, sharp enough to slit the hull of their craft.[29]

Ventress tells Dr. Sanders, "The disease is contagious, as you ask, yes, but years of exposure and contact are necessry for its transmission. The period of incubation may be twenty or thirty years." At first no one bothers about disease but after one year, it begins to spread viruses, whose nature is not exactly known. They infect human beings too. Viruses cause leprosy like disease due to crystalization of tissues. Experts visit the area of the forest to take samples and send them to Liberville. Military forces block passages leading towards Mount Royal. Dr. Sanders is permitted to enter the forest to treat the different people who are infected due to a strange disease of crystalization of tissues. He finds the crystalized body of the army captain, Radek. Ventress helps Dr. Sanders to save Radek but in vain. The half-crystalized body of men and women fuse against the trunks of the trees, the most of them are elderly couples seated together. In the summer-house, Thoreness, the mine-owner is crystalized. In the corpses, rigor mortis does not take place. The joints and tissues are malleable, the skin firm and almost warm. Dr. Sanders and his assistants find it difficult to control disease because of rapidity of spreading of the unknown viruses.

The consequences of the crystalization of tissue are desertion and emptiness in the Mount Royal area. Dr. Sanders observes:

> The streets of Mount Royal were deserted, and entire native population appeared to have long since vanished into the forest. The houses stood empty in the sunlight, shutters sealed across the windows, and soldiers paced up and down past the closed banks and stores. The side-streets were packed with abandoned cars, including that remedial river was the only route of escape from the town (88).

The remedial measures are undertaken to control the environmental catastrophe. The automatic temptation of the army is to seal off the entire area. Half a mile the road is sealed off by the lines of fifty-gallon drums painted with black and white stripes. The whole of the Florida peninsula in the United States, with the exception of a single highway to Tampa, is closed, and some million of the state's inhabitants is resettled in other parts of the country. Dr. Sanders states, "such is mankind's innate optimism, our conviction that we can survive any deluge or cataclysm, that most of us unconsciously dismiss the momentous events in Florida with a shrug, confident that some means will be found to avert crisis when it comes (103)." Here J.G. Ballard satirises mankind's false optimism which believes in withstanding with any environmental calamity. In *The Crystal World,* human hopes are dashed against the shores of reality and human efforts are futile to avert the environmental catastrophe. Human beings receive the mental shock and experience loneliness because of the failure of human efforts to cope with the calamitic situation. Beside the futility of human efforts, human relationships break in the grip of calamity. Dr. Sanders has affair with Suzanne for two years before coming to Port Matarre. But Dr. Sanders is posted at Port Matarre cannot revive his relationship with Suzanne. Isolation seems to be rule in the crystalized forest and it breaks relationship between them. Dr. P.S. Krishnamoorthy has viewed that *The Crystal World* is a picture of doomed world and it is "an account of a land disturbed by cosmic upheaval into crystalization with the result that its flora and fauna...humans included...are frozen in an eternal form."[30]

In this SF, landscape has psychological significance. A crystalization of forest is related to troubled mental state of Dr. Sanders. He has not one mind about Suzanne and his divided feelings are symptomatic of an even deeper ambivalence in his personality. He sees his love as a manifestation of the troubled mental state which strangly attracts him to leprosy : "Suzanne's sombre duty had become identified in his mind with dark side of the psyche, and their affair was an attempt to come to terms with himself and his own ambiguous motive" (22). Besides the relationship between the crystalized forest and Dr. Sanders, psychic state a deserted, an empty landscape is related to time and memory. A narrator says about the magical charm of the crystalized forest:

> A hubbub of speculation broke in the launch, during which only Dr. Sanders and Radek remained silent. The captain was gazing up at the over hanging trees, enconstructed by the translucent lattice, through which the sun light was reflected in rainbows of primary colours. Unmistakably each tree was still alive, its leaves and boughs filled with sap. Dr. Sanders was thinking of Suzanne Clair's letters. She had written, 'The forest is house of jewels.' For some reason he felt less connected to find a so-called scientific explanation for the phenomenon he had just seen. The beauty of the spectacle had turned the keys of memory, and a thousand images of childhood forgotton for nearly forty years, filled his mind recalling paradisal world when everything seemed illuminated by that prismatic light described so exactly by Wordsworth in his recollections of childhood. The magical shore in front of him seemed to glow like that brief spring. (85)

In childhood, everything is clothed in "celestial light, the glory and freshness of a dream," and crystalized forest is the paradisal world having a charm of dream. Dr. Sanders believes that illuminated forest in the same way reflects "an earlier period of our lives, perhaps an archaic memory we are born with of some ancestral paradise where the unity of time and space is the signature of every leaf and flower" (102). In the forest life and death have different meanings from that in our ordinary "lack-lustre world." He knows from his experience within the forest near Mount Royal that "all motions leads inevitably to death, and that time is its servant (103)." He has no assert that the process of crystalization which transforms the state of living tissue culminates into death, and time as a catalytic agent accelerates the process. A Landscape revives the memory in childhood and makes aware of a stark reality of death in human life. V. Gopman has aptly pointed out:

> Catastrophe—psychological, not physical—is really a metaphor, meaning a squall in human existence. The main thing for Ballard is to understand and show the tragic state of modern man's mind, his loneliness, his alienation, and his convulsive efforts to rescue his personality and keep it safe from the global cataclysms of the epoch.[31]

Here Gopman highlights the psychological significance of the catastrophic landscape and its bearings on modern man's mind. David Norman Samuelson in his doctoral dissertation, *Studies in Contemporary American and British Science Fiction*, has stated, "Ballard takes catastrophe less for its own sake and more as metaphor for the human condition, using obligatory scientific explanation."[32] The environmental catastrophe has a penetrating effect on the human psyche. Ballard has to show the psyche of a man who was going through the tragic changes in the age of an essentially new technology, an essentially new environment. Ballard's apocalyptic vision or reality is that environmental imbalance leads to disaster and the environmental catastrophe has bearings on psychic state of a man living in the age of science and technology.

Though catastrophic world which Ballard creates is bleak, it illumines the life of Dr. Sanders. Dr. Sanders mentions in a letter to Dr. Paul Derain, Director of the Fort Isabelle Traper Hospital:

> ...But what most surprised me, Paul, was the extent to which I was prepared for the transformation of the forest—the crystalline trees hanging like icons in those luminous caverus, the jewelled casements of the leaves overhead, fused into a lattice of prisms, through the sun shone in a thousand rainbows, the birds and crocodile frozen into grotesque postures like heraldic beasts caved from jade and quartz what was really remarkable was the extent to which I accepted all these wonders as a part of the natural order of things, part of the inward pattern of the universe. True, to begin with I was as startled as everyone else making his first journey up the Matarre River to Mount Royal, but after the initial impact of the forest, a surprise more visual than anything else, I quickly come to understand it, knowing that its hazards were a small price to pay for its illumination of my life. Indeed, the rest of the world seemed drab and inert by contrast, a faded reflection of this bright image, forming a grey penumbral zone like some half abandoned purgatory. (101-02)

Finding himself in a crystalized forest he feels that time is coming to a standstill and there, in the glare of the crystal trees and grass, something, he believes, will give meaning to his existence. And his perturbed and anguished soul is calmed. The sparkling light illumines Sanders's soul, and he believes that he has achieved inner harmony.

In this SF, Ballard deems environmental reality as a serious sign of a contemporary society. He stresses the tragic human condition in fantasy. Here fantasy seems to impart meaning and significance to reality. He poses a warning to human beings that environmental imbalance if not controlled may lead to a global disaster and can wipe out human existence on the earth.

VII

Clarke has attributed mythic dimension to SF. In his case, fantasy ceases to be fantasy and it becomes an imaginary tale which does not embody the elements of the contemporary world. He envisages the contemporary situation only to provide a flismsy support to an imaginary tale. 'Other World' which he imaginatively conceives does not confront the present world to view it in a new perspective. What is of seminal importance to him is not the present world but his vision which unfolds his meaning of reality. To Clarke, reality is not which we see in the outside world but it is within 'Other World' provides a necessary freedom to put forth a writers's vision of cosmos. He alleges that cosmos is inhabited by aliens which are intelligent and powerful. They have mysterious appeal. Human knowledge has limit and because of that it does not comprehend everything in a vast cosmos. He favours Stapledon's vision that the earth is a small planet in the context of cosmos and man is like a tiny speck. He satirises human egoistic thinking that human beings are only powerful intelligent beings in universe. Ballard has attributed the psychological dimension to SF. Fantasy points to reality in the present world more daringly to view it from a new angle. Fantasy stresses; magnifies; exaggerates reality to reveal a writer's meaning of reality. To him, fantasy is not turning away from reality but it is a powerful weapon to apprehend reality. Ballard's vision of reality is that universe has its natural order and if it is distrubed, it leads to disaster and human efforts in spite of progress in science and technology are futile to avert it. Environmental catastrophe poses a threat to wipe out human existence on the earth. It serves a curative function.

REFERENCES

1. New Worlds, March 1965; as quoted in the *Encyclopaedia of Science Fiction,* ed. Robert Holdstock; London: Octopus, 1978, p. 165.
2. Arthur C. Clarke, *Exploration in Space* (1951; rpt. Harmondsworth: Penguin Books Ltd., 1950), p. 185.
3. Arthur C. Clarke, *Childhood's End* (1953, rpt. New York: Ballantine Books, 1991), p. 193. (Other quotations are from this edition of the book and are indicated in parentheses by page number/numbers).
4. Arthur C. Clarke, *op. cit.*, pp. 26-27.
5. *Ibid.*, pp. 182-83.
6. Robert Scholes and Eric Rabkin, *Science Fiction: History, Science Vision* (New York: Oxford University Press, 1977), pp. 218-19.
7. John H. Timmerman, *Other World: The Fantasy Genre* (Bowling Green University Popular Press, 1983), p. 19.
8. Dr. P.S. Krishnamoorthy, *A Scholar's Guide to Modern American Science Fiction* (Hyderabad: American Studies Research Centre, 1983), p. 32.
9. Fredrick A. Krenziger, 'Popular Culture and People's Religion,' *Apocalypse and Science Fiction* (Chicago: Scholar's Press, 1982), p. 191.
10. Arthur C. Clarke, *Exploration in Space* (1951; rpt. Harmondworth: Penguin Books Ltd., 1950), p. 183.
11. *Ibid.*, pp. 187-88.
12. Arthur C. Clarke, *2001: Space Odyssey* (New York: William Heinemann Inc. and Octopus Books Inc., 1968), pp. 26-27. (All quotations are from this edition of the book and indicated by in parenthess by page number/numbers).
13. Robert G. Pieke, 'Star Wars vs 2001: A Question of Identity,' *Extrapolation,* Vol. 24, No. 1. Spring 1983, p. 147.
14. *Ibid.*, p. 152.
15. Rudoff Otto., *The Idea of the Holy* (New York: Oxford University Press, 1958), p. 10.
16. Quoted from V. Gopman, 'J.G. Ballard's Shattered World (Philosophical and Aesthetical Problems)', *Modern English Literature:* A Soviet View, Ed. Moisew Anatoli (Moscow: Progress Publishers, 1982), p. 385.
17. *Encyclopaedia Britanica*, Vol. 10, p. 374.
18. J.G. Ballard. *The Drowned World* (London: J.M. Dent and Sons Ltd., 1962) pp. 77-78 (All subsequent quotations are from this edition of book, and are indicated by page number/numbers given in parentheses).
19. V. Gopman, *op. cit.*, p. 386.
20. *Ibid.*, p. 385.
21. *Ibid.*, p. 383.

22. Dr. P.S. Krishnamoorthy, op. cit., p. 136.
23. V. Gopman, *op. cit.*, p. 386.
24. Quoted from James Goddard and David Pringle, ed. *J.G. Ballard: The First Twenty Years* (UK: Haynes. 1976), p. 31.
25. David Norman Samuelson, *Studies in Contemporary American and British Science Fiction Novel* (University of South California, 1969), p. 335.
26. J.G. Ballard, *The Drought* (1965: rpt. London: Johnthan Cape Ltd., 1984), p. 43. (All subsequent quotations are from this edition of the book, and are indicated by page number/numbers given in parentheses).
27. Lorenze J. Firsching. 'J.G. Ballards Ambiguous Apocalypse', *Science Fiction Studies,* Vol. 12 (1985), p. 304.
28. V. Gopman, *op. cit.*, p. 386.
29. J.G. Ballard, *The Crystal World* (London: Johnthan Cape Ltd., 1966), p. 85 (All subsequent quotations are from this edition of the book and are indicated by page number/numbers given in parentheses).
30. Dr. P.S. Krishnamoorthy, *op. cit.*, p. 136.
31. V. Gopman, *op. cit.*, p. 387.
32. David Norman Samuelson,. *op. cit.*, p. 343.

In Retrospect

In the modern time, SF came to be recognised as a distinct literary genre. On the one hand, SF points to fantasy, and on the other reality. The two elements, fantasy and reality chiefly control the thematic content of SF. Fantasy does not copy empirical world but creates a world which does not exist in empirial sense; it deals with the unkown, the unseen and the unfamiliar world. However, the term fantasy is not to be viewed reductively; it cannot be understood in the same sense. Reality, too, is understood in different ways. We cannot approach the relation between fantasy and reality in a fixed way. There is no reason why we should follow the preconceived notion about the inter-relation between the two in order to study British SF. To define a term is to impart fixity to it. Instead, the basic terms have been retained as open terms so as to know how different meanings grow round them. The major SF writers from 1890 to 1970 are H.G. Wells, Olaf Stapledon, Aldous Huxley, C.S. Lewis, George Orwell, Arthur C. Clarke and J.C. Ballard. The important task before SF writer is to make his fantasy acceptable to readers. In SF, fantasy is based on fantastic hypothesis supported by an established principle in science. But a rational ground of science does not necessarily make fantasy acceptable to readers as in the cases of Olaf Stapledon and C.S. Lewis. The SF writer invests the strange new world with human features and familiar details. What makes fantasy acceptable is its human core. Nothing serves so well for the authenticity of fantasy as the authenticity of human reactions to the events. While the land remains strange and unfamiliar, the emotions and feelings are maintained at the level of real. Once a fantastic hypothesis which has a rational base is motioned, the SF writer describes the 'other world' in a realistic way. In a general sense, fantasy is opposed to reason but in SF, fantasy is not opposed to reason. In the SF, fantasy and reason are complementary and this relationship constitute the heart of fantasy. In that world, what he relates is consistently true and it accords with the laws of this world and reader believes in it. In SF, a rigorous adherence to a fantastic hypothesis is important to make it credible.

We find that in the major British SF from 1890 to 1970 fantasy and reality are related in diverse ways. The SF writers, H.G. Wells, Aldous Huxley, George Orwell and J.G. Ballard have employed fantasy mode to extrapolate; to magnify; to stress the elements of the present world. Fantasy provides a necessary freedom to create the world which embodies the contemporary tendencies. Fantasy is not turning away from reality but it confronts with it more daringly to view it in a meaningful way. Fantasy points to reality. In SF fantasy is sometimes used as an efficient weapon to apprehend reality. Fantasy is at once both : means and end. Reality is not within but out.

In the cases of Olaf Stapledon, C.S. Lewis and Arthur Clarke, the relationship between fantasy and reality is tenuous. Fantasy, created on the assumption that it is "scientifically possible," does not necessarily have bearings on reality. This may, at the most, be treated as a writer's vision and there is no reason why others should not treat it as purely fictional. What is of seminal importance is not the present world but a writer's vision which unfolds the understanding of reality. Reality is that which a writer constructs. It is not what we see in the outside world but within.

The understanding of reality by different SF writers is different. Reality is not static but it is dynamic. It is meaningful; it is not absurd.

Select Bibliography

Primary Sources

Aldiss, Brian. *Barefoot in the Head: A European Fantasia.* London: Faber and Faber, 1969.

Ballard, J.G. *The Drowned World.* London: Golancz, 1963.

——. *The Drought.* 1965: rpt. London: Johnthan Cape Ltd., 1964.

——. *The Crystal World.* London: Johnthan Cape Ltd., 1964.

Brunner, John. *Stand on Zanzibar.* New York: Ballantine Books, 1976.

Burgess, Anthony. *A Clockwork Orange,* London: Cox and Wyman Fakemhan Ltd., 1962.

Clarke Arthur C. *Childhood's End.* New York: Ballantine Books, 1991.

——. *City and Star.* New York: William Heinemann Inc. and Octopus Books Inc., 1968.

——. *2001: Space Odyssey.* New York: William Heinemann Inc. and Octopus Books Inc., 1968.

Harlan Ellison. *Dangerous Vision. 33 Original Stories.* Garden city, N.Y.: Doubleday, 1967.

Hoyle, Fred. *The Black Cloud.* Harmondsworth: Penguin Books Ltd., 1967.

Huxley, Aldous. *Brave New World.* London: Chato and Windus, 1932.

——. *Island.* London: Cox and Wyman Ltd., 1964.

——. *Apes and Essence.* London: Chato and Windus, 1949.

Lewis, C.S. *Out of the Silent Planet.* London: Pan Books Ltd., 15th printing, 1973.

——. *That Hideous Strength*. London: Pan Books Ltd., 12th Printing, 1973

——. *Voyage to Venus*. London and Sydney: Pan Books Ltd., 1974.

Orwell, George. *Nineteen Eighty-Four*. London: Heinemann Educational Books Ltd., 1965.

——. *Animal Farm*. London: English Language Books Society, 1967.

Shelley, Mary. *Frankenstein*. New York: Potter, 1977.

Shute, Nevil. *On the Beach*. London: William Heinemann Ltd., 1970.

Stapledon, Olaf. *Last and First Men*. Last Men in London, (London: Cox and Wyman Ltd., 1932).

——. *Star Maker*. Harmondsworth: Penguin Books Ltd., 1973.

——. *Odd John*. New York: Doyer, 1972.

——. *Sirius*. London: Cox and Wyman Ltd., 1944.

Stevenson, Robert Louis. *The Strange Case of Dr. Jekyll and Mr. Hyde*. New York: Aeonian Press, 1976.

Verne, Jules. *Journey to the Centre of the Earth*. London: Hutchinson Educational, 1961.

——. *From the Earth to the Moon Direct and Round the Moon*. London: George Routledge and Sons, 1960.

Wells, H.G. *The Time Machine*. New York: Banton Books, 1982.

——. *The Island of Dr. Moreu*. New York: New American Library, 1977.

——. *When the Sleeper Awakes*. London: W. Collins Sons & Co. Ltd., 1921.

—— *The First Man on the Moon*. London: A.P. Watts Ltd., 1957.

——. *The Days of Comet*. London: Macmillan and Co. Ltd., 1906.

——. *War in the Air*. London: Collins Clear-Type Press, 1921.

——. *The World Set Free*. London: Collins Clear-Type Press, 1970.

Wyndham, John. *Chrysaldis*. Harmondsworth: Penguin Books Ltd., 1965.

Secondary Sources

Aauino Ohn. *Science Fiction on Literature*. Washington DC: National Education Association, 1976.

After Paul A. *The Creation of Tomorrow*. Columbia University Press, 1977.

Aldiss, Brian W. *Billion Years Spree*. New York: Doubleday, 1973.

Aldiss, Brian W (ed). *Introducing SF*. London: Faber and Faber Ltd., 1964.

Amis, Kingslay and Conquest Robert (ed.) *Spectrum IV and Fourth Science Fiction Anthology*. London Pan Books, 1967.

Apter, T.E. *Fantasy Literature: An Approach to Reality*. Indian University Press, 1982.

Asimov, Issac, Greenberg, Martin Harry, Olander, Joseph O. (ed.) *100 Great Science Fiction Stories*. New York: Doubleday, 1978.

Becker, George. *Realism in Modern Literature*. New York: Fredrick-Unger Publishing Co., 1980.

Bellamy, William. *The Novels of Wells, Bennett and Galsoworthy (1880-1910)*. London: Routledge and Kegan Paul Ltd., 1971.

Berger, Harold L. *Science Fiction and the New Dark Age*. Bowing Green, Ohio: Bowling Green University Popular Press, 1976.

Bleich, David. Utopia: *The Psychology of a Cultural Fantasy*. Ann Arbar, Mich: UMI Research Press, 1984.

Bretar, Herold. *Science Fiction: Today and Tomorrow*. New York: Harper and Row, 1974.

Bretnor, Reginald. *Science Fiction: Today and Tomorrow*. New York: Harper and Row, 1974.

Bretnar, Robert. *The Craft of SF.* New York: Barner, 1976.

Brooke-Rose. Christine. *A Rhetoric of Unreal: Studies in Narrative and Structure.* New York: Cambridge University Press, 1981.

Carter Paul A. *The Creation of Tomorrow: Fifty years of Magazine Science Fiction.* New York : Columbia University Press, 1977.

Chanady Amaryll Beatrice. *Magical Realism and the Fantastic.* New York and London: Garland Publishing., Inc., 1985.

Clareson, Thompson D. *Many Futures Worlds: Themes and Forms in SF.* Kent University Press, 1977.

Clareson, Thomas D. *Science Fiction Criticism: An Annoted Checklist.* Kent, Ohio: Kent State University Press, 1972.

Cleareson, Thomas D. SF. *The Other Side of Realism.* Bowing Green, Ohio: Bowing Green University Popular Press, 1971.

Colin N. Manlov. *Modern Fantasy: Five Studies.* New York: Cambridge University Press, 1975.

Cristophar, Joe, and Joon K. Osting (compiled), *C.S. Lewis: An Annotated Checklist.* Kent: Kent State University Press, 1960.

Davenport, Basil (ed.) *The Science Fiction Novel: Imagination and Social Criticism.* Chicago: Advent Publishers Inc., 1959.

Einstein, Albert. *Ideas and Opinions.* London: Alvin Redman Limited; 3rd edition, 1956.

Ellison, Harlon. *Dangerous Vision.* New York: Doubleday, 1967.

H. Bruce Franklin. *Future Perfect.* rev. ed. New York: Oxford University Press, 1978.

Frolov, Ivan. *Man-Science-Humanism: A New Synthesis.* Moscow: Progress Publishers, 1981.

Frye, Northrop. *Anatomy of Criticism.* Princeton, N.J. Princeton University Press, 1937.

Gerber, Richard. *Utopian Fantasy*. New York: McGraw Hill, New York, 1973.

Greenberg, Martin Harry and Worrik Patricia A. (ed.) *Political Science Fiction: An Introductory Reader*. Englewood Cliffs, New Jersey: Prentice Hall, Inc., 1974.

Gunn, James, Alternate Worlds: *The Illustrated History of Science Fiction*. Englewood Cliffs, N.J. Prentice Hall, 1973.

Gunn James (ed.) *The New Encyclopedia of Science Fiction*. New York: Viking, 1988.

Habegger, Alyred. *Gender, Fantasy and Realism in American Literarure*. New York: Columbia University Press, 1982.

Hall, H.W. *Science Fiction Book Review Index*. Detrait: Gale Research, 1975.

House, Key Seymour (ed.) *Reality and Myth in American Literature*. Greenwich: Conn Fawcett, 1966.

Hume, Kathlyn. *Fantasy and Mimesis: Responses to Reality in Western Literature*. New York: Methuon, 1984.

Jeffrey Meyers (ed.) *George Orwell: Critical Heritage* London: Routledge and Kegan Paul, 1972.

Ketterer, David. *New Worlds for Old: The Apocalyptic Imagination, Science Fiction and American Literature*. Garden City, New York: Anchor Books, 1974.

Knight, Damon (ed.) *In Search of Wonders*. Chicago: Advent, 1967.

Knight, Damon. *Turning Points*. New York: Harper, 1977.

Kroeber, Karu. *Romantic Fantasy and Science Fiction*. New Heaven Yale UP, 1988.

Lukas, George, *Eassays On Realism,* edited and introduced by Ridney Lingstone (and) translated by David Fernabach, Cambridge: Mass, MIT Press, 1980.

Melvin, Kenneth B., Brodsky Stanley L. and Fowler Raymond D. Jr. (ed.) *Psy Fi One: An Anthology of Psychology in Science Fiction*. Random House, Inc; 1977.

Moskowitz, Sam. *Explorers of Infinite: Shapers of Science Fiction*. Westport, Com: Hyperon Press, 1974.

Moskowitz, Sam, *Seekers of Tomorrow: Masters of Modern Science Fiction.* West Part, Conn: Hyperon Press, 1974.

Nicolos, Peter, (ed.) *Science Fiction at Large.* London: Gallancy, 1976.

Parrinder Patrick. *Science Fiction: A Critical Guide.* New York: Longman, 1979.

——. (ed.) *H.G. Wells: The Critical Heritage.* London: Routledge and Kegan Paul, 1972.

Peter Nicholas (ed.) *The Encyclopedia of Science Fiction.* London: Grandas, 1979.

Philip, Michael (ed.) *Philosophy and Science Fiction.* New York: Promethus Books, 1984.

Rabkin, Eric S. *Fantastic World: Myths, Tales and Stories.* Oxford Univ. Press, 1979.

Raghavacharyulu, D.V.K. *Utopia: The Quest and Crisis.* Waltair: Andhra University Press, 1965.

Raknem, Ingnald. *H.G. Wells and His Critics.* University of Forlaget: George Allen and Unwin Ltd., 1962.

Rottenstaner, Frany: *The Science Fiction Book : An Illustrated History.* London: Thames and Hudson, 1975.

Suvin Darko and Philmus Robert M. *H.G. Wells and Modern Science Fiction.* Lewisburg: Bucknell University Press, 1977.

Stern Willard, (translated) Erich Auerbach's *Mimesis: The Reproduction of Reality in Western Literature.* New York: Doubleday, 1957.

Scholes, Robert. *Structural Fabulation: An Essay on Fiction of the Future.* Motre Dame, University of Motre: Dame Press, 1975.

Subramanyam, N. *Movements in Modern English Novel.* Gwalior: Kitab Ghar, 1967.

Tuck, Donald H. *The Encyclopedia of Science Fiction and Fantasy Through 1968,* Vol. I (A-L). Advert, Chicago, 1974: Vol II (m-4). Advert, Chicago, 1978.

Wells, H.G. *Experiments in Autobiography,* Vol I. and Vol II. London: Victor Gollancy Ltd., and the Crescent Press Ltd., 1934.

Wolheim, Donald A. *The Markers: Science Fiction Today.* London: Gollanys, 1972.

Wollheim, Donald A. *The Universe Makers: Science Fiction Today.* New York: Harper and Row, 1971.

Journals and Periodicals

College English, Vol. 34, No. 3, December 1972.

Extrapolation, Vol. 22, No. 2, Summer 1981.

Extrapolation, Vol. 19, No. 1, December 1977.

Modern Fiction Studies, Vol. 17, No. 2, Summer 1971.

Modern Fiction Studies, Vol. 26, No. 1, Spring 1980.

Modern Fiction Studies, Anthony Burgess Numbers, Vol. 27, No. 3, Autumn 1981.

Science Fiction Studies, Vol. 3, Part 2, 1977.

Ibid., Vol. 5, Part 3, 1978.

Ibid., Vol. 9, Part 1, 1982.

Ibid., Vol. 14, 1987.

Ibid., Vol. 15, 1988.

Times Literary Supplements, 25th October, 1963.

M.Phil. Dissertation

Khandait, Naresh, *Fantasy Technique in Salman Rushdi's Novels,* Nagpur University, 1988.

Rukmani, Ranveer P., *Realism and Fantasy in the Novels of Kurt Vonneght Jr.* Osmania University, 1981.

Microfilms of Ph.D. Theses

Berger, H. Lynde. *Anti-Utopian Fiction of the Mid-Twentieth Century.* University of South California, 1969.

Samuelson, David Norman. *Studies in Contemporary American and British Science Fiction Novel.* University of South California, 1969.

Index

A

Absent, 9

Adliss Brian, 93

Aliens, 2, 6, 29, 78, 94-96, 99, 101-03, 105-06, 123

Allegory, 3, 13, 14

Alternative world, 12

Amis Kingsley, 4

Anxiety, 9, 21, 101

Apes and Essence (1948), 16, 38, 72

Apocalyptic vision, 34, 113, 122

Archetypal, 4

Asimov Issac, 14

Automation, 2

B

Bacon, 14

Bailey, J.O., 13, 48

Ballard, J.G., 93

Barefoot in the Head: A European Fantasia (1969), 93

Best Herbert, 71

Berger Harold, 130

Bloom Harold, 8-9

Bova Ben, 3

Brave New World (1932), 80, 88

Brodsky, Stanley L., 69

Brunner John, 93

Butler Saumel, 14

C

Cambell, John W., 4

Catastrophe, 14, 29, 32, 47, 67, 82, 108, 111-14, 116, 119-23

Caves of Steel, 14

Childhood End (1953), 14

Chrysaldis (1955), 93

Clareson, Thomas D., 10

Clarke Arthur, 79, 93

Cognition, 5

Consensus Reality, 12

Culture, 9, 42, 62

Cyclic History, 41-42

D

Dalton, 2

Darwin Charles, 38

Darwin Eramus, 2

Dystopia, 14-15, 72, 99

E

Eliotian sense, 15

Empirical, 5-6, 126

Empiricism, 15

Encylopedia Britanica, 107

Environmental, 46, 94, 106-08, 110-13, 116, 118-20, 122-23
Erone (1943), 71
Estrangement, 5
Eugenics, 37

F

Fantastic, 8-9, 19-20, 34, 38-39, 41, 55, 66-67
Fascism, 37, 47, 71
Fielder, Leslie A., 69
Fowler, Raymond D., 69
Frankenstein, 2, 18
Freud Sigmund, 17
From the Earth to the Moon, 34,
Futuristic, 3

G

Galvani, 2
Genre, 1-5, 10, 15-16, 38, 71, 78, 93, 106, 126
Gernsbag Hugo, 4
Glover, Donald E., 76, 78, 82
Goddard James, 125
Gopman, V., 108, 111, 116, 121-22
Gulliver's Travels, 14
Gunn James, 132

H

Haldane, J.B.S., 74-75
Hallucination, 7
Hammond, J.R., 92
Herrick Robert, 37
Heinlein, Robert A., 5
Hillegas Mark, 28, 89
Hitler Adolf, 84
Holsten, 30, 33
Hoyle Fred, 93
Hume Kathlyn, 12
Huxley Thomas, 2, 14, 16, 37, 71-72, 80, 99, 126

I

Imagination, 7, 9, 12, 22, 48, 74, 95, 101
Industrial Revolution, 1, 65
Invisible, 9, 108

J

Jackson Rosemary, 8

K

Kagarlitsky Yu, 25
Kalinga Award, 2
Kearney Chalmers, 71
Knight Demon, 24
Koch Robert, 62
Kreuziger, Frederick A., 99
Krishnamoorthy, P.K., 28

L

Lamark, 38-40
Last and First Men (1930), 16, 38, 42, 44, 46-48, 72, 74-75, 80
Lawrence, D.H., 6
League of Nations, 39, 41-42
Lewis, C.S., 16, 71
Linguistic, 8
Lundwall Sam, 3

M

Melvin, Kenneth B., 69
Mesmer, 2
Meyers Jeffrey, 88
Miller, 14
More Thomas, 14

Moorcock Michael, 2, 113
More than Human, 14
Morris William, 18
Moskowitz Sam, 5, 133
Mythology, 4

N

Naturalism, 13
Nazism, 37, 71
New world, 93
New Wave SF, 16
Nightmare, 4, 9, 37-38, 67, 83, 86, 89, 96, 108, 115
Nineteen Eighty Four (1949), 14, 16, 55, 62, 72, 83, 88-90

O

Origin of Species (1859), 38,
Orwell George, 16, 55, 61, 71, 126, 127
Otto Robert, 106
Out of the Silent Planet (1938), 16, 72-74, 77-79
Overpopulation, 2

P

Parrinder Patrick, 25, 28, 61, 88
Pavlov, 37, 57
Poe Edger Allen, 4
Pollution, 2, 113
Primary World, 11
Pringle David, 125
Psychoanalysis, 8, 111

R

Raghavacharyulu, D.V.K., 13
Realistic, 5, 10, 20, 73, 83, 126
Reason, 10
Redmayne, 30
Relativism, 15
Rogue Moon, 14
Romance, 2, 4, 9, 13, 19
Romanticism, 13
Rose Mark, 3, 27
Rubkin Erie, 54

S

2001: Space Odyssey, 16, 94
Sachapira J. Salwyn, 68
Safety Valve, 8
Sometime, 37
Satire, 13-14, 37, 66, 68
Samuelson David Norman, 14, 17, 112, 122
Scholes and Rubkin, 54, 82
Scholes Robert, 97
Scientification, 4
Scientific Fiction, 13
Secondary world, 11-12
Shaw Harold, 78, 82
Shelley Mary, 2, 18
Sherriff, R.C., 37
Shute Nevil, 93
Soddy Fredrick, 30
Spenglerian Theory, 41
Stalin Joseph, 84
Stand on Zanzibar (1968), 93
Stapledon Olaf, 16, 37
Star Maker (1937), 16, 38, 47-48, 54
Stevenson, 2, 18
Stream of consciousness, 6
Supernatural, 14, 47, 81, 90
Suvin Darko, 5

Swiftian, 88

Swinfen Ann, 11-12

T

Telekinesis, 12

Telepathy, 12, 46, 51

That Hideous Strength (1949), 16, 72, 79, 82-83

The Black Cloud (1957), 93

The Crystal World (1966), 14, 16, 94, 120

The Day of the Triffids (1951), 93

The Drought (1964), 16, 94, 113, 116

The Drowned World (1962), 16, 94, 106, 110-13, 116

The Hopkins Manuscript (1939), 37

The Invisible Man (1897), 18

The Island of Dr. Moreu, 18

The Lost World, 19

The Other World, 2, 56

The Poison Belt, 19

The Possible Worlds, 74, 79

The Strange Case of Dr. Jekyll and Mr. Hyde, 2, 18

The Time Machine (1895), 16, 18-19, 22, 25, 49, 72, 99

The Twenty Fifth Hour (1940), 71

The War of the World, 16, 18-19, 25, 28-29

The World Below (1929), 37

The World Set Free, 18-19, 30, 34

Timmerman, John H., 10-12, 58

Tolkien, J.R.R., 9-10

Totalitarianism, 71

Twenty Thousand Leagues, 34

Under the Sea, 34, 72

U

Unconscious, 4, 7, 110, 120

Unfamiliar, 6, 21, 35, 39, 41, 55-57, 67, 74, 83, 126

Unknown, 6, 11, 21, 28, 57, 101, 108, 119

Unseen, 6, 9, 28, 126

Utopian, 13, 24, 28, 33-34, 37, 43, 52, 68, 71, 75, 90, 94, 97-98

V

Verne Jules, 4, 13, 34, 72

Victorian, 1-2, 18, 24, 25, 29

Voyage, 14-15, 48

W

Walsh Chad, 46, 49

Wells, H.G., 1-2, 4, 13-14, 16, 18, 38, 126-27

Willing suspension of disbelief, 5

Wind From Nowhere, 94

Wish fulfillment, 3

World-1, 9, 12

Wright Sydney Fowler, 37

Wyndham John, 93

Atlantic
418/2/15 11/08
AJAY